# Pacification and its Discontents

*A "red-suspect" has been found hiding in the jungle and is now being questioned by the French Foreign Legion advance patrol who caught him. Vietnam, ca. 1954.*

# Pacification and its Discontents

Kurt Jacobsen

PRICKLY PARADIGM PRESS
CHICAGO

Prickly Paradigm Press, LLC
5629 South University Avenue
Chicago, Il 60637

www.prickly-paradigm.com

ISBN-10: 0-979-4057-8-5
ISBN-13: 978-0-9794057-8-5
LCCN: 2009936909


Printed in the United States of America on acid-free paper.

# Introduction

"Repetition compulsion" is a psychoanalytic term referring to the performance of an action again and again in order to gain relief from an earlier trauma by "getting it right" this time. The small abiding tragedy is that sufferers fail to achieve this mastery and instead become snared within a harmful behavioral loop that they neither can understand nor escape. Like all psychoanalytic concepts the term is properly situated in the experience of individuals, not of groups or institutions. Sliding carelessly over this individual/collective threshold is a common mistake that has spawned many a dubious, not to say idiotic, proposition.

Still, with all due reservations, there surely are social events that exhibit all the earmarks of repetition compulsion, even if they do get played out by major institutions in the domain of international politics. So especially there, where *Realpolitik* and the blooming buzzing confusion of reality meet, one needs to be acutely aware that there usually are alternative or overlapping "rational" or interest-driven sources of action. Nevertheless, international politics is at best only *partly* a rational enterprise to which psychoanalytic kibitzers therefore occasionally may have something useful to contribute. One such case is the 21st-century resurrection of counterinsurgency optimism. I say optimism is what is resurrected, not counterinsurgent practices, which never really faded away.

The refurbished US Army/Marine Corps *Counterinsurgency Manual* defines pacification as "the process by which the government assert[s] its influence and control in an area beset by insurgents," which includes "local security efforts, programs to distribute food and medical supplies, and lasting reforms (like land redistribution)." Who, aside from impudent insurgents, can object to these tempting treats? Yet pacification, as a linchpin of US strategy in the Vietnam War was responsible for the killing and maiming of untold numbers of non-combatants as well as of armed fighters who seem at times only to have gotten in the way. This widely ballyhooed strategy proved to be woefully counterproductive. "The more we won, the more we lost," observed war correspondent Jonathan Schell. "That was the paradox of Vietnam." Why? Because, in a nutshell, "our policies were destroying whatever support that [the South Vietnam] government might ever have had, which was probably about zero to begin with."

Judging from the upbeat references sprinkled throughout the *Manual* its avid authors beg to disagree. So Civil Operations and Revolutionary Development Support (CORDS), a coordinating committee of US Agencies formed in the Spring of 1967 with Robert Komer as Deputy Chief and then Chief, to stamp out the Southern Vietnamese resistance, is credited with "considerable success" in the intricate enterprise of modern pacification. A South Vietnamese Army (ARVN) brigadier general observed later that while "Blowtorch Bob" Komer displayed oodles of charisma, he was afflicted by a common bureaucratic ailment: an "obsessive preoccupation with appearances which led to the tendency of substituting statistical results for true achievements."

ARVN brigadier Tranh Vinh Tho, who was Assistant Chief of Staff for Operations, further notes that earlier the claim that 70 percent of South Vietnam pacified was closer to 10 percent in reality and that the weekly reports were "a matter of faith." In any case, the CIA, though a bit bashful about the extent of its role, was the key player running the pacification show

*CORDS Chief Robert Komer and Lyndon Baines Johnson meet in the White House in November 1967.*

through its crucial lethal stages. In practice, as scholar Jeffrey Race pointed out, the "developmental" and the "repressive" aspects of counterinsurgency action always fall under different agencies which invariably are at odds anyway. To establishment sages of that era and of the Bush II administration, this behind-the-scenes arrangement sounds as though the execution of US policies was in very good hands indeed.

For many sceptical Vietnam era beholders, however, the term "pacification," and its synonym "counterinsurgency," are stale euphemisms for violent suppression of popular resistance movements during superpower interventions abroad. This profoundly dubious approach was rehabilitated overnight inside a scrambling Bush II administration, and in much of the pliant mainstream press, as the occupation of Iraq malingered on, way past the hanging of that boastful "Mission Accomplished" banner. This time, just like the last time, chagrined authorities are determined to get it right.

According to the *Oxford English Dictionary*, pacification denotes "the condition of being pacified, appeasement, conciliation." A classic example is an "ordinance or decree enacted by a prince or state to put an end to strife or discontent." The verb "to pacify" means "to allay the anger, excitement, or agitation (of a person); to calm; quiet; to appease." More ominously, its meanings include: "to reduce to peaceful submission," as when the redoubtable Thomas Hobbes scribbled: "Counts ... were left to govern and defend places conquered and pacified." Who today fails to recognise the rueful Tacitus verdict about unstinting Roman retributive techniques: "they make a desert and call it peace," or else recalls, as Colonel Harry G. Summers reminds those of us with family Bibles at hand, the grim fate of the Midianites, as told in the Book of Numbers?

The strategy of pacification, under whatever cosmetic name, has been around as long as ambitious or desperate leaders have desired the ugly services it justifies. "Defenseless villages are bombarded from the air, the inhabitants driven out into the countryside, the cattle machinegunned, the huts are set on fire with incendiary bullets," George Orwell scribbled not so long ago in his classic essay "Politics and the English Language" about frankly imperialist policies. "This is called pacification." Counter-insurgency operations, according to Peter Brush in his study of Marines Corps activities, denote both "civic action *and* pacification programs and thus may be defined as 'the employment of military resources for purposes other than conventional warfare.'" Let us be sparkling clear. You don't pacify criminal gangs or nutty cults or bands of malcontents (e.g., the Symbionese Liberation Army goofs who kidnapped Patty Hearst long ago), you pacify entire populations who you know very well don't want you around. Who then still would want to get into this miserable business, and why?

In its 21st-century revival counterinsurgency doctrine is finely modified so as to be seen as a sagacious mix of enticement and coercion, as a discriminatory wielding of carrot and stick. Rather like a sepia-colored scene of a glowering 19th-century schoolmaster confronting a mischievous but promising pupil who needs to be tamed—always for his own good. The counterinsurgent agents, plunging into "remakes" of earlier situational psychic mayhem, need to imagine, if they have any glimmer of awareness at all, that they are fully equipped this time to surmount old painful barriers, such as, for resentful and petulant American elites, the "Vietnam syndrome," which discourages military adventures unless there is a clear national threat and full public support for action. What are bitterly resented by elites are any imaginable democratic barriers to acting as they see fit abroad.

Hence, a purely PR-motivated image must be peddled by insiders who see counterinsurgency as a solution to an Iraqi population that, however internally divided, overwhelmingly want the foreign schoolmasters to get the hell out. Far from tamping down insurgents, the unilateralist Bush strategy, according to the stuffy enough British International Institute of Strategic Studies, only functioned instead to boost the appeal of radical Islamists, and perhaps even within Western societies too, as the 7/7 bombings in London implied. Counter-productive again. But authorities, who see no downside in consequently aggrandizing power for themselves, invariably overstate the case regarding terrorism of the non-state sponsored variety.

Conservative romantics nevertheless assert that the US gave up too soon on the counterinsurgency catechism. One hardly could have blamed the US military anyway for a much-bemoaned "neglect" of pacification techniques, if such able scholars as Walter Laqueur deduced, after Saigon fell, that given the end of decolonization, potent insurgencies, insofar as they truly threatened states, were pretty much a thing of the past. Still, any rusty tool in a governing elite's coercion kit will be discovered anew whenever circumstances require it, though they always take on a gleaming new rhetorical gloss.

The reputed neglect of counterinsurgency is itself highly exaggerated, as even a glance of the *Manual* itself shows. In fact, counterinsurgency programs, unbeknownst to many outside military circles, and almost from the moment that the last American chopper fled Saigon, rousingly have been reinterpreted—in compensation, as Park Avenue shrinks might say—as a proud parade of heartening successes. According to cheery supporters, counterinsurgency, given enough "learning and adopting" to local milieus, will suppress armed opposition in Iraq, Afghanistan or anywhere, if only properly applied. If it does not work, it must have been improperly applied. That is all there is to it.

In popular culture one finds a "pulp" counterpart to this compulsive official optimism, as evident since the 1980s in a surge, so to speak, in fiction, movies and documentaries about Vietnam which focus obsessively and adoringly on "elite or special forces units." (No one watching the History Channel can possibly figure out on that pale booster-ish basis why the US lost the Vietnam War.) So the internalized siren song of repetition compulsion regains its voice among some resentful soldiers and most armchair militarists. Whether, given a set of circumstances, one ought to attempt a counterinsurgency campaign is a fussy sort of question that never arises in these bold accounts. We behold myriad task-oriented, no holds barred, "ours not to reason why" Light Brigade scholarship studies. Within the *Counterinsurgency Manual* one can root around all one likes and dig up only a brief for deploying a "learning organization" that, curiously, is forbidden to learn, or even mull over, certain lessons.

The bedrock credo of the *Manual* is crystallized in its solemn invocation of one Algerian War veteran's belief that "If the individual member of the organization were of the same mind, if every organization worked to a standard pattern, the problem would be solved." Does the *Manual* ever raise the question what the toll of the Algerian conflict over 1954-62 was for Algeria and for France? Certainly not. Martin Windrow in his study of Dien Bien Phu instructively wonders why: "Given France's own recent experience of occupation, murder, and atrocity, it is hard to understand how French officers—even setting aside all moral questions—could fail to grasp that this sort of behavior was self-defeating." The tragic answer is that, given the mission they were ordered to perform, they could not behave otherwise.

The *Manual* analysts are confined to, or besotted by, "mission fixation," a heel-clicking devotion to the parameters set by their masters. Once one has orders one merely enacts them just as did the *Wehrmacht* facing the maquis in France or partisans in Russia. Why pretend any contemporary situation is one iota different? If you cannot or will not question orders you are not someone whose arguments need to be taken seriously. This is what sober thinkers like to call a hard fact one must face up to. The exception to that hard fact, of course, is when the insistent arguer is armed and dangerous.

This pamphlet delves into the core of the *Counterinsurgency Manual*, reckoning the distance between its frothy ideas and ascertainable reality. So the Manual provides guideposts, even if it can be shown in the end to advocate nothing but wrong turns. Here I am less concerned with details of contemporary

*Wehrmacht troops interrogate a Soviet partisan in Russia, 1943.*

conflicts than with the doctrinal justifications and material interests driving rash US interventions abroad today. The Vietnam War is the crucial case for fervent rehabilitators of counterinsurgency who refashion its history to encourage modern applications. Insurgencies in Malaya, Central America, Northern Ireland and elsewhere are drawn into the argumentative fray, but everything in the rehabilitators' case hinges on Vietnam so it occupies the most space. Vietnam is still being fought today because the lessons we draw from that experience matter for the kind of nation the US is and will be.

# I: Mission Fixation

> Please leave your values at the front desk.
> —*Hotel sign in South Asia*

As early as 2004, as it became apparent even to some Dubya devotees that their devoutly wished mission in Iraq was not remotely accomplished, $3 billion of the appropriation budget was slated to gin up covert operations, with more funds coursing through various obscure pipelines. One didn't need a military genius, or the *Counterinsurgency Manual*, to tell you that the contemplated operations would strike not only armed Iraqi "rebels" and "foreign fighters"—as the Pentagon calls them—but also nationalist opponents of the occupation, including hitherto non-violent ones. The *Manual*'s conundrum is, "How do you eliminate the extremists without alienating the population?"

Mission fixation entails rigid assumptions that the chosen quarry is without merit, the passive population is unconnected to insurgents (except by intimidation), and that the government must be preserved at all costs. A boss or cabal occasionally may be ousted as a matter of expedience but replacements must align with US interests in all things. The "mafia model" of insurgency becomes the default mode for counterinsurgency strategists because it recasts all relationships into a framework of asymmetrically armed and extortionate gangs. Justice is a purely metaphysical nuisance, and is deemed not to be the counterinsurgents" business anyway. Reflecting on the justice, let alone practicality, of a given mission is not going to make it easier for counterinsurgents to accomplish it. This bluff attitude is applauded in prestigious policy circles as a "no nonsense" one.

The US public is urged to let crack military men and women, often barely out of their teens and getting by on 2 or 3 hours sleep daily for days on end, sally forth and "sort 'em out," a dog-eared *Manual* in one hand and a rapid fire Armalite in the other. Why, a psychoanalyst might ask the clench-fisted State quivering upon the couch, must you try so hard to relive painful memories? One rational retort, of course, is because foreign policy elites covet Middle East energy, but cannot say it so loudly that the easily swayed hoi polloi hear. The Project for a New American Century (PNAC) signatories, including virtually the whole upper tier of the Bush II administration, also aimed to shore up Israeli security, that is to say, Israeli domination in a region growing ever more volatile for that very reason. Reviving a pre-Vietnam sense of unbridled American military power would have been a treasured bonus. "The [Vietnam] war was not lost on the battlefield in any sense of the word," as Alexander "I'm in Charge Here" Haig, typically, complained. "It was lost in Washington."

Counterinsurgency in Vietnam came replete with a civic action dimension, with all the showy bells and whistles, on paper at least, explicitly pushing for the "nation-building" that George W. Bush ridiculed throughout his 2000 presidential campaign. Both military and civic action components customarily get lumped together in the definition of counterinsurgency as the "combined use of military resources for purposes other than conventional warfare." Perhaps the best known instance was the Phoenix Program, designed to wipe out—through assassination, kidnapping and torture—the leadership of South Vietnamese resistance, the National Liberation Front.

The standard alibi for the failure of US counterinsurgency strategy in South East Asia is that the Marines (or the CIA or Army special forces, according to different versions) had amassed an invaluable stock of fine-grained counterinsurgency wisdom over decades, but that this vital lore (whoops) had not for some inexplicable reason been brought to bear as it ought. Marine Corps commanders, for instance, complained about Army General William Westmoreland's attrition strategy, but, as Loren Baritz points out, the Marines wanted what was in effect already available—"unrestrained air operations and pacification." (Marine veterans testifying at the Winter Soldier Investigations in 1971 said that the unwritten rule for pacifiers was, "you can do anything you want so long as you don't get caught.") The animating faith is that violent techniques must be seen to work, regardless of the specific context or underlying superpower goals or the petty annoyances imposed by local power brokers. For all the *Manual*'s dainty pretensions to address local sensitivities, it ultimately is concerned about nothing but the application of crushing power, applied with the most, if not the best, intelligence available.

Former CIA counter-terrorism chief Robert Dreyfuss noticed early in 2004 that Dubya's administration was "clearly cooking up joint teams to do Phoenix-like things, like they did in Vietnam." The aim, as the *Manual* intones, is to create an indigenous security force to carry out counterinsurgency measures without need of intense external supervision, not unlike the Gestapo spurring the avid French police to round up the usual suspects, plus many unusual ones, in occupied France. So the CIA in Iraq was augmented by the elite military unit Delta Force and by the Navy SEALs, whose prime objective was to train reliable Iraqi law enforcement.

In Vietnam too the much-storied SEALs had instructed Provincial Reconnaissance Units (PRU), who were regarded by some observers as the best native troops—if you don't count the NLF. SEAL advisors reportedly accompanied PRUs on 15 missions a month on average in the late 1960s, just to insure quality control, one supposes, and perhaps of the kind former Senator and SEAL Bob Kerrey in 2001 undertook in a Mekong Delta village in 1969, killing many inhabitants either by mistake in a firefight or else in cold blood, depending on whom you care to believe.

In Iraq, native recruits were drawn from exile groups with long-nursed grudges to settle, but US forces also were not too shy to work alongside former members of Saddam's *mukhabarat* secret police. This super-pragmatic concession comes as no surprise to anyone acquainted with cold-blooded Cold War alliances between Free World spy agencies and former fascist organizations, such as Gehlen's Nazi intelligence apparatus. Secret policemen, after all, tend to have more in common with one another than with the citizens they purport to serve and protect. Marcel Ophuls made that point chillingly clear in his 1988 Oscar-winning documentary *Hotel Terminus*, re-examining the oddly lax hunt for Nazi war criminal Klaus Barbie. What Lord Acton said about power corrupting is doubly true for the secrecy so beloved by state agencies. No one operating in secret is entitled to anyone's trust, ever.

Up until his bum's rush exit at the end of 2004, late night entertainer and Defense Secretary Donald Rumsfeld gave secret commando units a free hand globally to strike at suspected terrorists, even though authorities freely admit that hazy intelligence often resulted in the wrong victim being fingered. Apparently, such mishaps don't even count as "collateral damage." The stalwart savants who authored the *Manual* clearly believe that the locals do not mind these grisly mistakes, or else they won't mind if they are handled with a firm but friendly hand. That is the single stellar lesson that self-labelled "revisionists" have extracted from the adamant insanity of the Vietnam war.

So an old gory story unfolds again. The need to square brute force with idealist objectives is what makes, in Marshall Sahlins' phrase, a "hardheaded surrealist" of anyone charged with the grotesque task. Images of American grunts with Zippos incinerating Vietnamese villages hark all the way back to the mass atrocities in the Philippines over 1898-1901, denounced at the time by the unsavoury likes of Mark Twain, who would have been grilled like a Summer sausage before a House

Committee on Un-American Activities had one existed at the time. (Twain's superb saturnine essay "To the Person Sitting in Darkness"—available on the internet—applies frightfully well to the post-9/11 hubris of Dubya's reign.) One may gallop further back for egregious examples of enlightened bloodshed to the gallant US cavalry sweeping the bountiful continent clean of meddlesome natives for the sake of Progress. Pacification of this sanctifying sort always required a sophisticated domestic propaganda apparatus to sustain it in practice.

States depend a great deal more than they like to admit on their power to define the sticky situations they often wade into. No one knows better how insidiously well this "power to define" works than does the generation who grew up playing war games and "Cowboys and Indians" in the post-war, pre-computer John Wayne movie era. Vietnam veteran Ron Kovic's childhood memories in *Born on the Fourth of July*—Norman Rockwell scenes bleed into and blur with Sergeant Rock comics—are shared by most impressionable males of his time, who in retrospect would guffaw at the notion that America was an anti-militarist nation. Those backward red-skinned and brown-hued natives of the 19th century may have had their merits; too bad they got in the way of implacable manifest destiny.

Go far enough West, though, and you wind up in the East, and exploits way out there become harder to explain away to a populace that was inclined to loath imperialism (at least, the epicene European overlord kind). In South East Asia the American authorities ultimately failed to make their customary rationalizations, or their dominance, stick. The rationale was selfless defence of the free world, even if the ring of defence had to be buttressed by a plethora of vicious police states. In the first few years of conflict after the Iraq invasion it also has been deemed the height of sophistication for news commentators to dismiss Vietnam analogies (not to mention the oil motive) as strident, puerile and overdrawn.

The all-purpose "war on terror" justification was pervasive in Britain, too, amongst what tabloids there call the chattering classes. Just a month before the Iraq invasion, I attended a jamboree of invited audience members for a special edition of *Question Time*, a national TV panel program, asking whether attacking Iraq would be such a brilliant idea. Before the main televised event, several hundred of us were divided into groups of a few dozen. My group's topic was: "Is oil the real motive?" In a face-off debate Scottish National Party leader (and now Scottish Parliament First Minister) Alex Salmond demolished a young Tory woman who preached that a maniacal Saddam could and would nuke the West any minute now.

But when audience members afterward were asked their opinion, all but my own hand ascended to signal a conviction that the motive for invasion was not oil at all. These people—businesspersons, economists and other credentialed professionals—were woefully easy marks for Tony Blair's allegedly nuanced arguments. None of them dared appear the least bit unsophisticated. As we filed out, a tall, silvery haired businessman, upon learning I was a Yank, apologized for Salmond's criticism of Bush, which he could understand in no other way than as knee-jerk anti-Americanism.

By the end of the next year, though, even pedigreed pundits were not so sure any longer that those simple-minded analogies to Vietnam did not hold in some important ways, or that oil was altogether irrelevant in the indecent haste to invade Iraq. Still, the bullying media propaganda war continued apace. Long before 9/11, anyway, Bush aides subscribed to the enticing fairy tale that pacification in Vietnam really had worked, so why not roll it out again? Bear in mind, as we continue, that often material circumstances—not intrapsychic impulsions alone—force patients into repetitions, although the reasons why these patients got themselves into the precise circumstances may bear closer examination too, both in terms of material interests in play and in terms of the psychic mechanisms facilitating their pursuit.

Sigmund Freud, after the outbreak of the First World War, remarked in a strikingly Realist manner,

> Psycho-analysis has inferred from dreams and parapraxes of healthy people as well as from the symptoms of neurotics, that the primitive, savage and evil impulses of mankind have not vanished in any of its individual members, but persists, although in a repressed state, in the unconscious [and] It has further taught us that our intellect is ... a plaything and tool of our instincts and affects. If you will observe what is happening in this war—the cruelties and injustices for which the most civilized nations are responsible, *the different way in which they judge their own lies and wrong-doings and those of their enemies and the general lack of insight which prevails*— you will have to admit that psycho-analysis has been right in both these theses. (Italics mine)

Indeed.

One thing that the *Manual* surely is not is a free-ranging discussion tool. It lays down its own double-standard law unequivocally. Perspectives of any other faint-hearted sort are alien to it. The old parodic paradigm bursts into full, unblushing bloom: "We are freedom fighters; you are rebels; those swarthy guys over there are terrorists." The *Manual* therefore informs us that the task of the targeted insurgents "is to break the ties between the people and the government," as if such ruptures only occur as a result of terrorist coercion. An article of faith for state managers is anointed as the whole truth and nothing but. The insurgents also are said to attract, and themselves become (if they are not already) criminal elements. This mingling can happen, but even so it does not always supersede the broader causes driving a conflict. In Indonesia in 1945-46, as British forces aided the restoration of hated Dutch colonial rule over a resistant population, historians Christopher Bayley and Tim Harper note in their volume *Forgotten Wars*:

> Many of the more organized and politicized *pemuda* militias made common cause with the underworld of large cities such as Jakarta to draw on the expertise of men experienced in violence. The *bersiap* amounted to social revolution in some areas—in north and east Sumatra the old aristocracies came under bloody attack—but in Java much of the republican leadership fought shy of its implications; here the social revolution remained a feral population, without programme or direction. In many places it simply meant a struggle for scarce resources or settling of old scores. "The Indonesia revolution," admitted the Islamicist leader Abe Hanifah, "was not totally pure."

Encountering nationalist resistance, the British, in a little-known action in November 1945, nearly leveled the city of Surabaya, killing as many as 15,000 people. Purity is not to be had in politics, as Burkean conservatives are first to tell you. Neither then are the motives and tactics of the civilizing colonialist powers so very admirable. The history of governments hiring criminals to do their dirty work, especially abroad, is an extensive one, ranging from Nazis appointing criminals as kapos in concentration camps to the CIA hiring mafia hit men to assassinate Castro to the numerous drug-peddling deals sanctioned to fund US covert operations around the globe. Likewise, the history of beleaguered governments "criminalizing" political

*An Indian soldier uses a knocked out Indonesian nationalist tank as cover in a main street in Surabaya during the fighting, November 1945.*

opposition is as old as governments themselves. (Northern Ireland in the 1970s and 1980s experienced such a cynical and counterproductive episode.) What we behold among self-described revisionists is a collective case of convenient projection, unhindered by historical referent.

Counterinsurgents, the *Manual* exhorts, must strive to avoid imposing their idea of normalcy upon a leery foreign culture. In practice this sensitive edict usually means that the counterinsurgent authority will allow itself to resort to the most vile loopholes in foreign law—someone else's normalcy—in order to suit its own purposes, as has the Bush II administration in its proliferation of rendition flights to foreign prisons (initiated, as the Bush administration accurately retorted, by Bill Clinton) for purposes of enhanced, uninhibited interrogation. One of the secret pleasures of "emergency" situations for authorities, as any psychoanalyst can tell you, is that they gain license to behave as badly as they please, and do so with an almost orgasmic sense of self-righteousness.

The *Manual* is chock full of distressingly dubious data, which ought to put any savvy reader on guard. It claims, for example, that the Provisional IRA made extensive use of religious iconography, a claim concocted by Ulster sectarian authorities themselves in a manner reminiscent of the Czarist secret police manufacturing the Protocols of the Elders of Zion. If anyone resorted to religious iconography for political purposes in Northern Ireland, it was desperate Protestant Loyalists who reacted violently when the subjugated Catholic population in the mid-1960s dared to march for "equal rights for equal British citizens." One wonders about the skewed sources of information since only a dolt, a cynic, or a partisan would believe that religious supremacy was ever what was at stake in the long Ulster conflict.

## II. Rehabilitating Vietnam strategy:
## The Pentateuch of the Pentagon

The Vietnam revisionists' case hinges on a self-crafted "ironic" view that counter-insurgency triumphed at the instant an American withdrawal got under way. "We" won, but foolishly bugged out anyway. Here is a bracing modern wrinkle on the "stab in the back" stories that accompany every loss by a great power. The consoling implication is that military strategy and performance were sound, and only required more time for necessary fine-tuning to kick in to rescue a valued pliable ally. This interpretation got great play in powerful US circles, and rose unabashedly into public view in the early 1990s, with another boost after George W. Bush was inserted by Supreme Court fiat into the oval office in 2000. The thrilling assumption is that there really was a sane way to win the Vietnam War without obliterating the population, going nuclear, or expanding the conflict into

China. I zero in on five authors whose rehabilitative works comprise what amounts to the Pentateuch of this rehabilitative movement. These authors and their volumes are, in no particular order, Mike Moyar's *Phoenix and the Birds of Prey* and *Triumph Forsaken*, Zalin Grant's *Facing the Phoenix*, Lewis Sorley's *A Better War*, Harry G. Summers' *On Strategy* and William Colby's *Lost Victory*.

Moyar's saga of the Phoenix program is laced with jaw-dropping implausibilies, blithe contradictions and tendentious arguments. Moyar teaches at the US Marine Corps University in Quantico, Virginia, where faith in counterinsurgency doctrine never flickered. This study is, to say the least, imaginative and provocative. Mass murder can be "an effective counterinsurgency tool," even if you bump off a lot of people who were trying to mind their own business. Moyar argues that the early Strategic Hamlet program had not disintegrated during Diem's regime but was doing just dandy—yet admits that by 1964 the struggles in the villages "were almost all on the Viet Cong's side." Moyar soundly points out that Lyndon Johnson could have gone either way in 1964-65 on the question of full-scale Vietnam intervention, but once in, for whatever reason, one goes all the way. That, you see, is the only reasonable thing to do.

According to Moyar, the local and evidently low-IQ rustics understand if high-spirited authorities bump off the wrong guy every now and then, so long as it is done with the best intentions and in a good cause: "Allied uses of violence ... were aimed primarily at Communist soldiers inside the hamlets, rather than at the hamlet residents. The villagers appreciated this factor and attached considerable importance to it." The fact that such shoddy wishful thinking as this screed can be regarded as fair and balanced in academic circles is truly disturbing. In 2006 Cambridge University Press published Moyar's follow-up, *Triumph Forsaken*, which trumpeted that Diem was a "very wise leader," the key Buddhist demonstrations of 1963 were communist-led, that strategic hamlets worked like a charm, the domino theory was valid (which it must be for his analysis to matter at all), Ho Chi Minh was not a nationalist, and that Vietnam was "a wise war fought under foolish conditions."

Moyar cannily portrays his retouch epic and those of kindred "Light Brigade scholars" as heartily revisionist. So it is only the stuffy old orthodox school that views the war as "wrongheaded and unjust" while audacious champions of the revisionist school, like Ronald Reagan, see it, unblinkered, as a "nobler but improperly executed enterprise." These "revisionist" verdicts are far better described as figments of the reigning orthodoxy in place before curious scholars began to take a sceptical look at the expanding war.

One longs for bygone days when shy authorities at least tried to hide their complicity in torture and assassination. "[T]orture was indeed used," Moyar admits, but then those wayward South Vietnamese allies always "were the despair of Americans for killing every suspect turned up." One mustn't fret unduly about victims, though, because the often lethal techniques were used "almost always against hard-core Communist cadres and soldiers rather than civilians of uncertain loyalties." How on earth does Moyar know this for sure? And why is it okay under those circumstances? He implies that Americans today, as well as way back then, are just helpless bystanders while our *Fu*

*Manchu* foreign allies congenitally mistreat their captives. "American advisors today face the same dilemmas of whether to object to brutality against prisoners," Moyar claims, "as they again are given the conflicting requirement of respecting allied nations" sovereignty and discouraging their counterparts from violating Western rules of war." Overstepping the moral boundaries is always the fault of those inscrutable aliens. George W. Bush later opted to redraw, if not erase, all boundaries.

The insurgents maliciously mingled with the population (with whom they are allowed to have no other conceivable bonds) in what Moyar believes is a violation of the Geneva Convention, which therefore evokes eminently excusable violations in reprisal. Who can blame crack counterinsurgent forces for getting carried away whilst purging unscrupulous foes who won't fight fair and in the open? So denial and projection "walk point" hand in hand throughout this po-faced, jingoist genre. State terror is the whole point. The Phoenix programme Moyar so gamely defends was devised to enable the US military to attain a gruesome "crossover point," where NLF dead and wounded exceeded the movement's ability to replenish itself.

During Nixon's first two and a half years, the State Department reported that Phoenix eliminated or abducted 35,708 Vietnamese civilians—a lowball estimate. Ex-Phoenix agents testified that orders were given to kill South Vietnamese Army, and US military personnel, who were considered, on almost anybody's say-so, security risks. Criminology professor David Currie, for example, while an officer in US Army Intelligence monitoring Phoenix radio traffic, told me how shocked he was when he first heard orders delivered to kill several ARVN soldiers whose capital crime was to support a non-communist political rival of Thieu.

Due process was, despite William Colby's perfunctory expression of concern before a 1971 Congressional Committee, absent. ("Out here," Colonel John Wayne sneered in the sun-sets-in-the-East 1965 movie travesty *The Green Berets*, "due process is a bullet.") Barton Osborn, a CIA case officer in the Phoenix program, told Congress, "I never knew an individual to be detained as a VC suspect who ever lived through an interrogation in a year and a half." Phoenix was not remotely calculated to court hearts and minds—except insofar as US and GVN "black teams" sneaked out dressed in enemy gear, with their ensuing assassinations and mayhem to be blamed on the NLF.

The Phoenix Program employed CIA assassination squads. The main counter-terror teams were called the provincial reconnaissance units (PRUs). "Technically, they did not mark cadres for assassinations," *New York Times* reporter Neil Sheehan notes in *A Bright Shining Lie*, "but in practice the PRUs anticipated resistance in disputed areas and shot first. People taken prisoner were denounced in Saigon-held areas, picked up at checkpoints or captured in combat and later identified as VC." If you weren't an NLF sympathizer before being nabbed you likely would become one afterward, providing you survived the ordeal and were not permanently crippled. In her archival study of Army investigations during the War, Deborah Nelson cites an intelligence officer with the 173rd Airborne brigade who testified "that any VC sympathizers he potentially found would be targeted for death." More humdrumly, the "ticket punchers"—opportunist careerists who are legion in any organization—turned a blind eye to brutal interrogations, and frequently participated.

"The crime of Phoenix was not the use of harsh methods to apprehend or destroy the enemies of the GVN," Douglas Blaufarb assesses. "Its crime was ineffectiveness, indiscriminateness, and, in some areas at least, the violation of the local norms to the extent that it appeared to the villagers to be a threat to them in the peaceful performance of their daily business." Like Moyar, he suggests that the "Americans involved erred in not appreciating the extent to which the pathology of Vietnamese society would distort an apparently sound concept. The GVN was guilty of both misfeasance and malfeasance in executing the program."

Yet let's return to Schell's account of the fate of a flattened village site during pacification festivities in 1966: "You could say that the operation came off beautifully. It worked exactly as planned. The helicopters flew in, moved the people out, destroyed the village. Mission accomplished, But to what end?" Schell asks. "The unmistakable fact was that the general population despised the United States, and if they hadn't despised it before we arrived, they soon did after we destroyed their villages..." Was only the GVN guilty of extraordinary "misfeasance and malfeasance" in the energetic conduct of otherwise well-plotted operations?

Moyar, like other devout "revisionists," asserts that in the "overwhelming majority of cases the people whom Allied forces eliminated were found with weapons or incriminating documents in their possession." So most of the 385,000 civilians he modestly estimates were killed must have been toting AK-47s and RPGs. On the other hand, one finds that the 9th Infantry Division in the Mekong Delta during "accelerated pacification" over the first half of 1969 reported an "official body count of 11,000 with only 748 captured weapons." What gives? One searches in vain in the *Manual* for the clinical word "massacre," and for a cool pragmatic discussion of its indispensable and unavoidable role in protracted counterinsurgency campaigns.

## III. Beyond the Measure Principle

By 1967 the NLF shifted their strategy in some districts where they avoided patrols they formerly ambushed. Government intelligence. according to Brush, reported that the NLF decided no longer to fight "pacification efforts. Rather, the guerrillas were to gather intelligence and act as guides and reinforcements for the main forces." This shift made sense both before and after the 1968 Tet offensive. The NLF alone couldn't overcome the vast apparatus of American forces, although they would have toppled the Diem government, had it been unaided. By 1969 the CIA too concluded the North decided to avoid major engagements in order instead to fill the porous GVN government with spies—possibly 30,000—so that Thieu's regime could crumble from within. Post-war accounts are rife with stories of American veterans and correspondents discovering that trusted South Vietnamese aides turned out to be NLF agents. "There is probably not one government army unit, camp, public agency, or even ministry without its share of Viet-Cong informants," judged Swedish journalist Kuno Knoebl at the time. Not even Moyar seems to believe that friendly Iraqi zones today are any less riddled with spies, informers, and double agents.

Moyar asserts that the villagers shifted to whichever side served their interests, and could inflict more punishment upon them if they didn't. The villagers therefore blamed horrific shelling on the VC, not on trigger-happy ARVN or US forces. The villagers, who would have to be recklessly suicidal to defy the desired government narrative, dutifully told official inquirers that they deplored the VC for bringing upon them nothing but ruin. ("You heavily armed guys asking these dumb questions are okay.") Moyar strains to affirm everything that the authorities wanted the villagers to believe, but sometimes a stray fleck of truth does slip through. "The villagers only blamed the GVN when their attacks weren't justified," is a moment that is incontestably true. Millions who were forced to become wretched refugees wisely blamed their mounting misfortunes entirely on the wily VC, or so goes the official refrain.

Moyar points confidently to young Vietnamese men who allegedly enlisted to fight against the disloyal NLF, although most of them were forced by impressments or poverty into the military and paramilitary services. In a South Vietnam nation of 18 million people, 1.1 million men were conscripted into military service and another 4 million served in local security units. This condition constitutes security? About a million tons of US/GVN ordnance saturated South Vietnam over 1969 and 1970 alone. That is security? Moyar treats the struggle as nothing but a competition between two bands of gangsters (theirs and ours) for the right to exploit a prized turf. This movieland portrayal handily expunges all questions of justice, of social values, of nationalist aspirations. One can easily see why this pseudoscientific framing is, for state managers then and rational choice modelers today, drop dead gorgeous.

Another zealous rehabilitator of the pacification gospel is Zalin Grant, whose *Facing the Phoenix*, the publisher's blurb proclaims, is based on the shrewd reckonings of a South Vietnamese master spy, whose foolproof plan to defeat communists by community action "was perverted by the CIA." According to the NameBase website, Grant assiduously argues that

> certain players had a good handle on how to neutralize the enemy through local political action and enlightened aid programs. Just as they were making significant strides, however, they were thwarted by corruption in Saigon and by big-bang, big-bucks conventional-warfare mongers like William Westmoreland.

So then, if only "we" had disposed of the crummy regime "we" were defending, and the US military high command who were defending it, "we" would have won.

Call a psychiatrist, please.

These reveries constitute perfectly logical thinking in high policy circles today. Lewis Sorley likewise asserts that "accelerated pacification" under William

Colby's direction from November 1968 onward was a stirring success. Sorley estimates that upwards of 465,000 South Vietnamese civilians were snuffed, and that, startlingly, "many of them [were] assassinated by Viet Cong terrorists or felled by the enemy's indiscriminate shelling and rocketing of cities"—a level of firepower remarkably tantamount to the colossal American/SVN levels. How did those crafty runts smuggle all those back-breaking heavy munitions down the Ho Chi Minh trail while the US was striking its snaking passageways with as much high explosive as was expended in all of World War II?

Sorley says that the war "was being won on the ground even as it was being lost at the peace table and in the US Congress." Rational debate, for these diehard "revisionists," begins only when one concedes that the US could have—and by implication, should have—won the war. General Westmoreland's strategy foolishly emphasized the attrition of North Vietnamese Army (NVA) forces in a "war of the big battalions." Sorley's hero, General William Abrams, on the other hand, "wisely emphasized not the destruction of enemy forces per se but protection of the South Vietnamese population by controlling key areas—a unified "one war" strategy which would have saved the day—at least until the next day.

Sorley, oddly, waters down his own case by drawing our attention to the potent April 1968 Mini-Tet, the August/September "Third offensive," and subsequent actions spurred by the NLF, who seem embarrassingly aggressive for an extinct organization. This unseemly robustness accords with a CIA analyst who, after Tet, "also noted that although the enemy suffered heavy losses, their forces appeared to be regrouping and could mount further large-scale action in a matter of weeks." The furtive enemy, according to this subgenre, is always on the run, and we always are about to roust them from their foul lairs in this devastated, defoliated, defiant land. Just one more big push is all it requires. Here is rampant repetition compulsion, which, as I mentioned in the case of collectivities, need not be divorced from frank pursuit of material goals.

Moyar asserts that by 1970 sincere Americans, through magnanimous Land-to-the-Tiller reforms, won over wary Vietnamese villagers—villagers who forgave the Americans and GVN forces for countless murders, maiming, "relocations," arrests, and rough treatment because they were confident that the blundering authorities meant well. This image of the ordinary ingratiating Vietnamese is yanked straight out of an imperial era *Boys' Own* magazine. It is an ideological convenience born of a rulers' top-down perspective, imposed regardless of skin tone of the imposer or the imposed upon. "Most of the South Vietnamese had a very simple dream," gamely explained Colonel Nguyen Van Dai, a Commandant of the GVN's National Police Field Forces. "They wanted to have peaceful lives and to not worry about having food. They didn't want to be afraid of someone capturing them or torturing them or killing them. They supported anyone who could bring peace for them." Would any police chief anywhere say anything else?

The villagers naturally were "attracted by military presence and strength," Moyar says, and so the "use of highly destructive weaponry in the villages" resulted in a "weakening of communists and an increase of support for Americans." This perplexing behavior apparently occurs because a renowned feature of modern warfare is that grieving victims of violence usually rally to the side of their oppressors—rather like Stockholm syndrome writ large. How can anyone who is not overpaid or ordered to do so take this preposterous rubbish seriously for a millisecond? The Vietnamese—or Afghan or Iraqi—peasant necessarily is depicted by these staunch "revisionists" as a primitive, apolitical and childish being, but one who is just rational enough to be obligingly amenable to the highly credentialed analyst's rational means of persuasion. It stands to reason, at least in certain intellectual precincts.

Coincidentally in late 1940s Malaya, as Bayley and Harper note in their study of *Forgotten Wars*, clever British officials deduced from the get-go that the primarily ethnic Chinese "support which [the communists] get is almost wholly through intimidation and cannot by any stretch of the imagination be described as 'popular'... The truth is the Chinese are accustomed to acquiesce under pressure." Coincidentally too one can find sober reports bristling with identical estimates filed just about every place an insurgency ever occurred. Malayan pacification—held up as a model of accomplishment—actually soaked up about half the annual public budget and required a decade and a half of police state measures, forced mass relocations—not to mention "seven British infantry battalions, eight Gurkha battalions, three 'colonial' battalions and the Malayan Scouts, two Royal Armoured Corps regiments, ten RAF squadrons, two Royal Australian Air Force squadrons, and a small naval contingent"—and a good deal of unacknowledged luck. The notion in the Malayan case "that 'winning hearts and minds' was a carefully prepared strategy is a myth," Bayley and Harper conclude:

> The classic manual was written—by Sir Robert Thompson, an ex-Chindit, Chinese affairs officer and later secretary of defense in Malaya—only after the Emergency was ended. At the time the strategy was "an agglomeration of trifles," and it proceeded mainly by trial and error. Many of the aftercare measures, as they were termed, arrived in fits and starts sometime after the worst effects of resettlement—the uprootings, banishments, loss of income, exposure to corruption and exploitation—had already been experienced by the rural Chinese.

Moyar nonetheless quotes the same Sir Robert Thompson to pronounce about Vietnam in 1972 for once and for all that "the VC side of it is over. The people have rejected the VC." John Paul Vann, engaging clay-footed hero of Sheehan's *A Bright Shining Lie*, likewise is quoted by Moyar as judging from deep inside one of the most vicious police states in the world that miraculously 95 percent of South Vietnam residents prefer Thieu's regime to any other imaginable government. Moyar, like all these disgruntled revisionist cheerleaders, also invokes the solemn article of faith that Linebacker II, the 1972 Christmas bombings of North Vietnam, really "won the war."

This enchanting establishment myth brushes aside the plain fact that nothing was gained by the bombings—when the US suffered nightmarish aerial losses—except to help to coax Thieu into signing onto the ragged peace deal. What Nixon got after the Christmas bombings from the allegedly cowed enemy was exactly what was on offer before. "Air power, marvelous in its flexibility," analyst Earl Tilford sums up the ironic situation, "had succeeded in bombing an ally into accepting its own surrender." Still, that violent tack also handed the addled American Right an invaluable consolation prize—the means for bragging ever afterward that it bombed Hanoi to the peace table, which is apparently all it ever wanted to do.

While we are on the subject of bombing civilian centers, Meyers notes that the giddy claims by the Air Force to have achieved "increasingly accurate targeting owed a great deal more to the shelter and evacuation procedures of the [North Vietnamese] population." In fact, "three quarters of Hanoi's population was evacuated during air attacks. Barry Romo of Vietnam Veterans Against the War, who was in Hanoi with a civilian peace delegation, including Joan Baez and Telford Taylor, during the Christmas bombings, told me of visiting a nearby North Vietnamese town which clearly had been obliterated by the "pinpoint" attacks. Romo recalled that Telford Taylor, an upper crust Nuremburg Trials prosecutor, was in tears that Americans could deliberately do such a thing. Estimates of the tonnage of the ordnance dropped on all of Southeast Asia, including Cambodia, Laos, and Vietnam, vary from 7.8 million tons to 15 million tons. Whatever the correct figure, comparison with past wars emphasizes the great magnitude of the Vietnam air war: for example, the US and its allies dropped "only" 2.7 million tons of bombs on the greater land mass of the European, North African, and Asian theaters during World War II and 678,000 tons of bombs on Korea. A lot of devastated Vietnamese villages and towns, North and South, must have gotten in the way of hitting precisely calibrated targets.

## IV. Hokum and Taboo

Another celebrated rehabilitator is Colonel Harry Summers, whose book *On Strategy* argued that US leaders were led astray by a "new model of Communist revolutionary war." The mischievous influence of half-baked experts such as Sir Robert Thompson, you see, "channeled our attentions toward the internal affairs of the South Vietnamese government rather than toward the external threat." The Americans therefore concentrated on puny Viet Cong guerrillas, leaving powerful North Vietnam forces comparatively unscathed. The guerrilla war was entirely a waste of energy. Summers, who readily admits the First Indochina War "was a revolutionary war," says that "expending military resources on inconclusive military and social operations" during what the Vietnamese call the "American war" exhausted the "patience of the American people."

*A Viet Cong prisoner awaits interrogation at the A-109 Special Forces Detachment in Thuong Duc, 25 km west of Da Nang, Vietnam, January 1967.*

The American military, made of infinitely sterner stuff, could have gone on and on if only the objectives had been sensible and clear and unanimous.

The US objective, contrary to Summers' depiction, clearly was to sustain Thieu's regime, period. Revolutionary war theory, as John M. Gates notes, never ever implied that the guerrillas "achieve decisive results on their own," although Gates omits to mention that even by US estimates the NLF would have overthrown the Southern regime had America not contrived the Gulf of Tonkin incidents and soon afterward poured in hundreds of thousands of ground troops. One acute personal irony of the war is that Navy pilot John Stockwell, one of the first POWs and therefore longest imprisoned, flew overhead that night and knew very well that no attacks on US ships had taken place.

Gates expresses surprise as to how non-Communist leaders of the NLF ever believed they "were working for Southern self-determination and independence—from Hanoi as well as from Washington," as Summers too rather reasonably assumes. Yet almost from day one civic action, Brush rebuts, remained distinctly a sideshow to US efforts to wage a more congenial conventional war, which it was better prepared to wage. Anyway, the "US was perceived as the ally of the GVN; the civilian population saw neither government as an ally. The more the US took control of the war to avoid the defeat of the ARVN by the Communists, the greater the ability of Hanoi to portray the US as neo-colonialists and the GVN as a puppet regime."

The NLF called for peaceful reunification, eventually—rather like Sinn Fein in Northern Ireland. "In retrospect, knowing the tremendous casualties taken by the Communists in the course of their resistance since 1945, one cannot even assume that the destruction of the DRV's conventional military power would have ended the war," Gates judges. "The history of conflict in Indochina and the continuation of the fighting long after the United States withdrawal indicates that the physical conquest of the DRV base in the North might have been needed to destroy the Communist will to continue the war." Summers, in his introduction to Moyar's *Triumph Forsaken*, says that the Viet Cong were the "War's ultimate loser." So too does Noam Chomsky, but for very different reasons.

Arch-rehabilitator William Colby in *Lost Victory* follows this unvarying revisionist story line: "The ultimate irony was that the people's war launched in 1959 had been defeated, but the soldiers' war, which the

United States had insisted on fighting during the 1960s with massive military forces, was finally won by the enemy." One almost senses Colby's lips curling as he writes the loathsome term, "people's war," which has no business frustrating a bona fide superpower. (Soviet Generals and spooks doubtless experienced the same form of dyspepsia about Afghanistan during the 1980s.) Colby complains that reports of rip-roaring successes in the countryside after 1969 were not adequately publicized—for information and how it is interpreted is the prime concern for cool intelligence mandarins such as Colby, who goes on to compare the fall of South Vietnam to the fall of France in 1940, as if they were equivalent tragedies.

The "accelerated pacification campaign," which Colby directed, "was a great success" and "the basic objective of increasing the population living in security from the enemy was indeed achieved." Colby touchingly assumes that the tired, huddled, strafed and bombed masses, burnt out of their homes and manhandled by government forces, were yearning to be free only of the VC. Since 1968 the Phoenix program, to that end, "captured 29,978 communist 'leaders'" in the Viet Cong infrastructure, 17,717 more had taken advantage of the amnesty program, and 20,587 had been reported killed, "mostly in combat situations." These grisly stats bring up an interesting question.

If there were thirty thousand admitted "leaders," then just how many followers are we talking about? A very ticklish question that goes emphatically unasked. Precisely "87.6 percent of those killed were killed by regular or paramilitary forces, and only 1.4 percent by police or irregular forces." How do you manage to kill so many people who you supposedly are looking for under guise of civil/police authority? Don't inquire. The PRU and local militia fought "superbly," although Colby concedes that they were guilty of numerous atrocities. For Colby, nonetheless, "the fact that Phoenix was reducing the arbitrary way the war was being fought was lost in the impression of wrongful death." As for the delicate matter of day-to-day operational responsibility, President Thieu set up a Central Pacification and Development Council to oversee the carnage, but "we Americans had no apologies for putting huge pressure on officials" to see and do things our way.

Colby oversaw the trembling human traffic in special centers in each of South Vietnam's 44 provinces, each special center constructed with CIA funds. Colby manfully admitted that serious abuses occurred. He did not know how many innocents the Phoenix program killed. Maybe 5,000. Maybe more. In response to a Congressman's question: "Do you state categorically that Phoenix has never perpetrated the premeditated killing of a civilian in a non-combat situation?" Colby sincerely replied: "No, I could not say that. I certainly would not say never." It was all in a good cause.

CORDS reported that from January 1968 through May 1971 exactly 20,857 insurgents were killed. The GVN more freewheelingly boasted that it had notched up 40,994 surgically precise assassinations from August 1968 through July 1971. According to those impeccable CORDS statistics, 12.4 percent of enemy losses were attributable to the meticulous meat-grinding machinery of the Phoenix program. Kenneth Osborn, a former Phoenix operative, however, remarks that this best-laid scheme quickly had degenerated into little more than a "depersonalized murder program."

So sweeping a counterinsurgency program undeniably inflicted heavy losses, even on armed enemies, whilst spawning more enemy replacements. In some parts of South Vietnam, a majority of *identifiable* NLF activists allegedly were killed, caught or driven into hiding. The figure is easy to credit, given that so many non-NLF members were killed too. Phoenix, a State Department publication said, had set a target for 1969 of eliminating 1,800 alleged VC per month—which left, and invited, a lot of room for error. Guesswork of this macabre sort is what agencies such as the CIA are most adept at, and dependent upon, imposing on others, even upon their legal monitors. Some academic observers do credit a drop in VC support after 1968 in hard-pressed regions—from 80 percent pro-VC to 50 percent—but note that support for the government never exceeded 15 percent.

Intelligence agencies are especially coy about loot. When asked in Congress about the minor matter of 1.7 billion missing dollars, Colby regretted to inform the House subcommittee that he did not have authority to discuss the perilous reasons why they could not audit what, after all, are taxpayer funds. Had a welfare mother been implicated in the unaccounted-for funds, Congress surely would have pried further. The $8 billion reported missing early in the corporate bonanza known as the Iraq war set neither a precedent nor perhaps, when inflation-adjusted, a record either. For some of that Vietnam investment, however, GVN police detention centers diligently "processed" some 180,000 people annually to defend democracy.

The US funded a national identity registration project where absolutely any Vietnamese age 15 and up was jailed if they did not flash a credible ID card on demand. Contemporary security junkies will deem some of the missing billions well-spent on such a promising pilot program overseas, for the whole thrust of the 2003 Patriot Act is to treat Americans who can't or won't join a Republican country club as incipient insurgents too. In Vietnam a state-of-the-art RAND computer tabulated 15 million suspects, cross-linked to 10 million paper dossiers, photos and fingerprints. One might imagine that the extraordinary burden of tracking 15 million suspects, the vast bulk of the Southern population, might have given a few agents pause to reassess the very sanity of the expensive war they were fighting. Thousands of low-level Foreign Service Officers in the South East Asia section resigned their posts during the Vietnam War.

Reconsiderations of this radical kind appear to have been taboo, though, in higher political and military realms where career ambition trumps scruples almost every time. The US/GVN intelligence services pooled avalanches of utterly fallible data together with misbegotten news flashes from informers and prisoners so as to guide police and paramilitary activity in extinguishing even the unlikeliest threats to the regime. No South Vietnamese citizen minded the intrusions or terminations with extreme prejudice; at least, none complained to Colby or Moyar.

Humble rural folk luckily "showed little or no inclination to join the insurgents." Given these heartwarming testimonials, one has to wonder why authorities bothered with cumbersome ID systems and other menacing gimmicks. But one can't be too careful. Colby even invokes the brutal Japanese relocations in the US during the Second World War in order to justify massive forced migrations in Vietnam. As for winning hearts and minds, a University of Washington professor designed the basic land reform package that the US promoted in the Philippines, Vietnam, and later in El Salvador. The minor flaw in it is that in every case the program accompanied, or ignited, state-sponsored "rural terror: in Vietnam, the Phoenix Program; in Philippines, martial law; in El Salvador, a state of siege." Colby, like Sorley, strays momentarily from the rightwing songbook when he acknowledges that in 1968 "the Communists mounted another surge of attacks during the coming months to try to pick up the momentum the initial Tet attack had lost." Really? But weren't the NLF already reduced to pathetic tatters?

Regarding *Pentagon Papers* revelations of what amounted to mandatory White House mendacity, Colby "had no real problem with their accuracy;" it's just that "their coverage ended in May 1968 just when CORDS had begun its work." Colby, by some hermetic process of elimination, cannot help but attribute the loss of Vietnam to the anti-war movement—a point addressed further on. The 1972 Christmas bombings, thank goodness, were "precise and effective," even though the US took heavy aerial losses, a mutiny brewed among B-52 bomber crews, and no gain whatever in negotiation terms was made for the US/GVN. Vietnam was a defeat of "the entire learning process we went through there," Colby laments. "After years of trial and much error, we had finally learned how to meld our military, political and economic efforts in support of a single strategy and of a unified mechanism for its execution." This burlesque is the "learning process" that the *Counterinsurgency Manual* so piquantly propagates.

Colby displays all the indignant fury of the Brahmin administrator who, having done everything right and with the requisite light touch, is compelled to watch helplessly as it all goes horribly wrong in some-one else's klutzy hands. For a clinching anecdote to illustrate successful pacification procedures, Colby recalls his stunt one day in 1969 chauffeuring nationally syndicated newspaper columnist Stewart Alsop down a former VC-controlled road and impressing Alsop with the absolute safety they enjoyed, which is an exhilarating tale repeated elsewhere often in the pro-war literature. Former General Douglas Kinnard, though, supplies a rather different take on Colby's amazing journey:

> In 1969 *Newsweek* carried a story by Stewart Alsop in which he waxed enthusiastic about an unescorted automobile tour he took with [CIA director of rural pacification] William Colby from Ca Mau to Can Tho in the Delta. The fact that they could drive safely in this area was billed as an example of the impressive gains in pacification. What Alsop didn't know was that they actually had a large military escort. Armed teams and helicopters preceded and followed the car just out of sight.

In his study *War of Ideas* former Army Colonel Robert W. Chandler, scrutinizing the contorted propaganda dimension of the war, makes some wise allowances for jubilant claims about the Phoenix Program in improving overt civilian behavior. Nonetheless, "the corruption, the heavy-handed treatment of the civilians, the torture and imprisoning of innocent persons, and the use of the [Phoenix] program to disguise political repression of non-communists outside of the Thieu government doubtlessly destroyed much of the good will created by the pacification effort." That is to say, as the flailing pacification machine rolled remorselessly forward its achievements rolled back up right behind it—like a tropical steamroller which, except for carpet bombing, is as blunt an instrument as one may deploy.

The questionable purposes of the counterinsurgency campaign go unexamined while the motives ascribed to the resistance are little more than pure projections of one's own side's unsavory motives. "Peasants were attached to private property"—which the Saigon regime did not provide them with much of, except under duress—and these simple folk had no truck whatever with "abstract ideas like nationalism and communism." Still, Colby patricianly cautions, they were "poorly educated and easily swayed by demagoguery"—unlike, say, a considerable chunk of the US public who dutifully swallowed every official lie about the conflict right down to its ignominious end. Colby repeats the complacent cynical refrain that villagers simply sided with whomever had the upper hand, which is a *de rigueur* tenet for purveyors of McNamara era systems analysis and of what later came to be called rational choice theory.

Rational choice is derived from a profoundly context-bound image of the way that human minds actually work. Fair enough when applied with ample humility, but formal frameworks invariably generate extremely irrational behavior when practitioners are insensitive to, or ignorant of, their intrinsic context-dependence. The *homo economicus* assumption underlying rational choice would not prove to be a particularly helpful one for sussing out the nature and aims of the insurgency. In Vietnam the local combatants on both sides of the 17th Parallel regarded the typical Western equation of what is real with what is countable (body counts, tonnage dropped, sorties flown, money wasted) as a very violent form of modern mysticism. Number-crunchers like to believe they are not mystical.

What was overlooked by oblivious imperious analysts—apart from all the discouraging data—was what Robert Jay Lifton in his book *History and Human Survival* called an over-spilling of "disintegrative tendencies into the realm of idea systems and images [causing] a breakdown not only of social institutions but of the shared symbols necessary to ordered existence—symbols defining rhythms of life and death, group loyalties, and the nature of reality." Rationalist reward-punish models favored by policy makers utterly misunderstood the history, motives and strategies of their opponents. What invariably gets lost in these cramped, circumscribed analyses is the connection between normative ends and instrumental means.

A rationalist model, by deprecating the qualitative phenomena of culture or social psychology, frustrated the very aims for which it was intended to be the most effective means to success. One might have somewhat more confidence in hard-nosed realists if they were not inclined to such startling misjudgments as the belief that America lost the Vietnam war "due to deficiencies of our ally" and declaring that culture is irrelevant because the NVA and Viet Cong, on one hand, and the South Vietnamese army, on the other, "were products of similar strategies and political cultures." Gabriel Kolko in *Vietnam: Anatomy of War* punches home the point:

The functions, actions, and values of officers and soldiers are the inevitable consequence of the kinds of societies they are seeking to create or defend. This social context defines the character of the officer corps and the soldiers, their relationship to each other, and their human, social and economic impact on the population. Strategy mirrors this reality and in turn weighs strongly on the balance of forces. This framework exerts an overriding influence on soldiers' motivations in battle and an army's ability to endure protracted war. In this vital regard the Vietnam War was from its inception a very unequal battle between radically different kinds of armies.

Eqbal Ahmad had it exactly right in 1970 when he surmised in a *Bulletin of Concerned Asian Scholars* essay that rationalist analysts "were unable to recognize that a government that was totally dependent on a foreign power is inherently lacking in legitimacy." So instead the mission-fixated technocrats must resort to "a systematic distortion of the facts" in order to carry on their assigned dirty work regardless. This technocratic approach was embraced uncritically by high-level policy legionnaires "more concerned with order than with participation, more with techniques of governing than with the consent of the governed, more with stability than with change." People are the "mere objects of policy." When optimism about counterinsurgency doctrine was resurrected in 2003, so too were all these funhouse mirror attendant attitudes.

# V. All in Their Heads

In 1932 Sigmund Freud expressed his total opposition to war, "because everyone has a right to his own life, because war puts an end to human lives that are full of hope, because it brings individual men into humiliating situations, because it compels them against their will to murder other men..." Freud, unlike many esteemed and well-rewarded figures, declined to attribute warfare to instincts run amok. Indeed he saw some room for improvement in realizing one's enlightened self-interest and thereby avoiding wars. Belligerence was not inscribed in our genes. The waging of war, even Freud noted, usually tallied with self-interest in some way even though it emanated as well from, and reached into, psychological depths too, which warranted investigation.

A "can-do" spirit surely has its place in the military, but in both academic scholarship and intelligence analysis it is an unfailing source of distortion. George W. Bush's White House established an Office of Special Plans, and other disinformation units, to generate advantageous distortions in data in order to mislead Congress and the public (as if *New York Times* reporters at the time needed any assistance). If the President or the CIA director tells you, as an employee, what you must find, what else can you do (except whistle-blow and/or resign)? Why, however, do scholars often buckle under to official views? Well, for one thing, there is highly remunerative work for PhDs willing to tell their preening hard-line bosses what they want to hear.

An American Psychological Association member attempted to cajole it to sanction members who aid and abet military interrogations. He concludes that the leadership was reluctant for fear of losing a lavish source of funds plus quite a cozy relationship with military and intelligence agencies stretching back to the CIA's MK-Ultra programs and beyond. Psychologists served in Behavioral Science Consultation Teams at Camp Delta at Guantanamo and at other "black sites," and were involved in every aspect of interrogations. In May 2006 the American Psychiatric Association stated that under no circumstances should psychiatrists take part in such activities. In August 2007 the American Psychological Association voted down a similar ban, although the next year a candidate for the APA presidency ran on the platform of ceasing such repulsive cooperation.

A suffocating managerial mentality comes into play among for-hire shrinks and scholars who accept the edicts of policy elites and thereafter assume that they perform laudable scientific tasks. One international relations "scientific" axiom is that wherever resistance arises, more than proportionate force must be deployed, and moving up the scale swiftly to "shock and awe." Force, moreover, must be seen to work in the eyes of the relevant domestic audience, even if it really doesn't do so on the ground. Here is the conformist mindset Noam Chomsky found pervaded the "new mandarins" of the Vietnam era: devout, cold-blooded, hard-nosed, numerical and officious. These semi-scientific heel-clickers were then, and are today, pleased to comply with urgings from the top to convert "a pleasing hypothesis into a fact"—which, as Hannah Arendt reminds us, is a highly fecund source of official lies.

Confronting US/GVN atrocities in Vietnam, the routine response is that they (the NLF/NVA) did it too—ignoring that "they" didn't do exterminatory things at a level anywhere near the high-tech US scale, and that they didn't harm Americans who managed to chill out in Little Rock or Oxford or the Texas and Indiana National Guard for the duration. This outpouring of rehabilitative revisionist studies especially has been welcome grist for the mills of rational choice—a direct heir of 1960s era systems analysis. The squishy "soft" issue of social justice (because not measurable to the third decimal point) cannot appear adequately within the crisp conceptual boundaries of formal theory, and therefore values do not matter much, except as window dressing. Searching for "keys under lampposts" (where the theory is all that sheds light) is a dismaying academic tribal conceit that bleeds into life and death policy matters abroad.

The resurgent case for counterinsurgency relies on a great deal of suspiciously warmed-over data, such as the US Hamlet Evaluation Survey, which was conducted by government agents in 1970-71 and has been re-evaluated later by David Elliot, formerly of the far from impartial Rand Corporation, in his study *The Vietnamese War: Revolution and Social Change in the Mekong Delta, 1930-1978*. The fact that these superficially punctilious evaluations rely on agencies that were catering to counterinsurgency objectives—and that information was extracted under life-threatening duress—does not seem to register or else is acknowledged briefly and then tactfully never mentioned again as the analysis proceeds along with scholarly aplomb.

Hence, in the 21st century one again may draw upon cooked-up evidence to dispense the comforting conclusion that "every quantitative measure we have indicates that we are winning this war" (as Robert McNamara opined in October 1962), in order to support the required moral lesson that the brawny US

*Photo taken by US Army photographer Ronald L. Haeberle on March 16, 1968 in the aftermath of the My Lai massacre showing mostly women and children dead on a road.*

can stomp puny foes. Yet even in the most ideological organizations, uncooked data does sneak through and is taken note of, though rarely to the career benefit of the quixotic analysts who do the noticing.

"McNamara now says we didn't know anything about Vietnam and what was really happening was not understood," said Evelyn Colbert, formerly of the Southeast Asia Division of the Bureau of Intelligence Research at the State Department in the 1960s. "That's a lot of garbage. We would come out with papers showing that things were going very badly indeed. But the record shows that dissent which contradicted the public optimism was ignored." A former CIA analyst in Saigon attests that there was "no shortage of Southeast Asian specialists in the foreign affairs and intelligence wars of the US government." The problem was that, if the news were jarring or unpleasant, "the consumers did not want what they were producing."

McNamara was "was caught up in a dream of power that substituted the databases of a preferred fiction for the texts of common fact," Lewis Lapham incisively writes in *Waiting for the Barbarians*. "What was real was the image of war that appeared on the flowcharts and computer screens. What was not real was the presence of pain, suffering, mutilation, and death." McNamara since has done public penance, however imperfectly. (See Errol Morris' documentary *Fog of War* and my review "The Passion of Robert McNamara, or Sympathy for the Devil?" in *New Politics*, Summer 2004.) There is a touching, old-fashioned, nagging conscience evident in McNamara's life that is utterly absent in members of the Bush II administration, with the possible exception of Colin Powell. Fresh and unchastened pre-Vietnam McNamara mentalities proliferate, as they will wherever there is a demand for their lame-brained, lickspittle form of schoolyard brilliance.

## VI. Hearts and Hectares

The Hamlet Evaluation System rated A, B and C as "secure." D and E were "contested." V was "enemy controlled." Would anyone here prefer the lattermost lethal ranking? Hardly anyone except a few "revisionists" bothers to deny that indiscriminate aerial and artillery bombing raked areas deemed to be controlled or even occasionally visited by the pestilential NLF. The incentive structure was stark and plain. The way local agents responded to the incentive structure was not so plain. Elliot shows that even when the NLF "lost" a village due to pacification it usually maintained a foothold in mini-bases nearby. Former Army officer Frank Maguire, an infantry officer with three tours of duty, interviewed in Christian Appy's oral history on Vietnam, said: "One of my jobs was taking the figures from the HES reports and turning them into briefing charts. I remember the time a colonel and I sat up one whole night with a bottle of scotch, not changing the figures but moving them around and labelling them so it would turn out we were winning the war. And in those days after Tet it looked like we were."

Maguire further recalled:

Another indication of where the war was going was the Hamlet Evaluation System (HES). One day I saw my radio operator, Foley, with this huge print-out—the HES report. I said, "Let me see that". They had all sorts of questions as to the attitudes, intentions, political leanings of every hamlet in the district. I said, "Foley, where do you get the information to answer all these questions?

He said, "Oh I just fill it in." I looked at it and said, "You say everything in the district is fine."

He said, "Yeah, I always do." Then I said, "Foley, "You say here there's no VC within two hours of this location."

He said "Yeah?"

Foley, there's no place in this whole damn country where there isn't a VC within two hours. When you go out the gate and into An Khe town, do you take a .45 with you?

He said, "Do you think I"m crazy? Of course, I do."

So I changed the report and within seventy-two hours I was on my way to Saigon explaining why I had downgraded the evaluation. I met the youngest full colonel I'd ever seen. He was a computer nerd and it was his absolute conviction that when he finished his plan he would be able to predict what was going to happen anywhere in Vietnam, at any time. I said, But colonel, what you're dealing with are my guesses. My guesses become your facts."

He said, "Well. We have a factor built in to take care of that."

Statistically hypnotized people always do.

One of the favorite tales resuscitated by the Vietnam rehabilitators is that the vaunted "Land to the Tiller" program won villager hearts in grateful droves. The program was implemented well after the Staley Plan "strategic hamlet" catastrophe of the early 1960s. The basic premise of the strategic hamlets "was that the peasants wanted to resist communist infiltration but were powerless to do so," a European correspondent observed. "Unquestionably, many peasants wanted security from the Vietcong because they knew that the moment they fell into the hands or submitted, the government would strike back." They had no reason to love a government that was so careless with their lives and livelihoods.

The "Tiller" myth, in any case, ignores three things: first, great swathes of South Vietnam already were under NLF control; secondly, land there had been redistributed; and thirdly, the Thieu reforms were neither redistributive nor popular. The US administration obligatorily lauded "land to the tiller," but the record belies this achingly smiley-face story. In the 1950s eighty percent of peasants in the Mekong Delta were tenants while just 1 percent owned 44 percent of the fertile rice land in all of South Vietnam. The first land "reforms" of the Diem government, Mark Selden notes, actually restored to delighted landlords the properties parcelled out by the Viet Minh before the 1956 partition.

By 1960 the NLF redistributed 77 percent of arable land in My Tho province. (The first visitors after

US/GVN forces secured each village, it was caustically noted, would be thrilled absentee landlords collecting back rent.) The "tiller" program featured a Stolypin-like emphasis upon creating a solid collaborative class of well-off "middle" peasants. But the distribution of uncultivated land in insecure areas (littered with scads of unexploded ordnance and trigger-happy patrols) required capital if the land was to be restored to use, for which only usurious private loans were available, as Ngo Vinh Long observed. As elsewhere, this inherently exploitative situation invited a reconcentration of control of property. The weak Thieu reforms could not compete with the extensive real redistribution organized by insurgents. As the NLF expanded areas of control, it became increasingly difficult for the landlords to collect rents. They therefore struck a fateful bargain with their government: the army would collect the peasants' rent in return for a 30 percent cut, which was to be split three ways between the government, the officers and the troops. Rent collection became more important to the army than fighting. The seamy South Vietnamese government and its army were little more than tax collectors for the landlords. The enormous economic and military power of US imperialism was no stronger than the social relations of its corrupt and reactionary colonial clients.

Under the severe pressure of "accelerated pacification," the cadres "holed up in briar patches, recuperating and waiting for better times"—which came around in 1971 and again during the Spring offensive of 1972. Tax revenues for the NLF fell for a while but rose again in 1971. The NVA forces in the South too were dependent on the NLF for guidance. The so-called pacified areas often survived because of tacit quid pro quo arrangements. They were used by NLF cadres for what amounted to R & R spots in exchange for not rattling the cages of government agents stranded there, who valued their skins and therefore went "though the motions." A modus vivendi was attained in some areas where villages thus escaped shelling and other mayhem while GVN agents—when they weren't double agents—safely wielded daytime authority.

"What the Pentagon describes as 'secure areas' in Vietnam," Kolko aptly summarizes, were "often a staging and economic base as secure and vital to the NLF as its explicitly identified liberated zones." Even more so, nod and wink arrangement apparently were worked out latterly in the war as well between some American units and the NLF. One also had to "question if so many enemy personnel had rallied [defected to the Southern regime] or been eliminated, how could the [Viet Cong] continue to pose a permanent threat to the pacification effort," a former ARVN General, who complained of a "live and let live" attitude prevailing in rural areas throughout the war, asked himself long afterward. "Indeed if statistics were useful, they strongly indicated the enemy's capability to recruit and replace surpassed everything we usually attributed to him."

US monitors claimed that US/GVN forces controlled 67 percent of South Vietnam on the eve of the 1968 Tet Offensive. The same sources assert that US/GVN control soared afterward. The reports the pacification enthusiasts relied upon were equivocal at best, and, often enough, contradictory. Moyar mentions flaws riddling the HES system but nonetheless reverts to saying it "did track a positive trend." Yet Elliot found that the Mekong Delta area he studied was "strongly pro-VC" in 1969-70, well after the Tet offensive had supposedly killed off the majority of guerrillas, not to mention the innumerable lethal Phoenix forays (including "license to kill" Tiger Force operations) and 9th Infantry division sweeps. Elliot noted that few locals "defected from the war effort."

Studies by Bergerud, Trullinger, Pace and Werner and Hunt likewise testify that the districts they studied overwhelmingly favored the NLF in 1964-65 when the US ground troop escalation began, and remained high through all the bloody ups and downs of the war. Without question, the NLF was hit hard during and after Tet. Still, Komer, CORDS director, afterward admitted, even if granted the best case regarding NLF attrition, "we were never able to translate this into positive and active rural support for the government of Vietnam." The truth is that sullen acquiescence would be perfectly fine with authorities who could not help but employ burgeoning state terror to fight what they liked to define as terrorism. High on the list of official achievements in this regard, or so rehabilitators reckon, is the bloody culling work of the local Territorial Forces, the Regional Forces/Popular Forces (RF/PF), commonly called ruff-puffs, who comprised half of South Vietnam armed personnel. "They were the local militia-men too old or too young for the ARVN, soldiers retired or medically discharged from the ARVN, and yes, deserters who had become worn out by years of service in the ARVN and who just went home but were still willing to carry a gun to protect the local populace," explains US General Frederick J Kroesen. The "ruff-puffs" are credited with inflicting 30 percent of NLF/NVA casualties but themselves incurred well over half the government casualties.

A South Vietnamese general recalls that one of his "constant headaches came from requests for reinforcements from field commanders who always asked for more and never seemed to be happy to settle for less." This was perhaps an indication of RF and PF ineffectiveness. He writes:

> Somehow I got the impression that pacification was like a leaking tank. No matter how much manpower you put in it, it never seemed to be enough for the task... ARVN was spread thin in its attempt to fill in the void where territorial forces were incapable of maintaining security. The enemy was thus given the chance to infiltrate local activities because many areas were left undefended for lack of forces...
>
> ...In the Mekong Delta the VCI was successful in transforming several RF and PF soldiers into turncoats. As for GVN cadres, [their] abuse of power and for personal benefit and the pursuit of worldly pleasures were widespread. Cadres were not always ideologically motivated; many of them were materially motivated.

Two other ARVN generals, General Cao Van Viem and Lt. General Dong Van Khuyen, in a jointly authored study reflected:

> Experience indicated however that in due time those enemy units which had been destroyed were surfacing again. Apparently they had been regrouped, refitted, and reorganized in base areas with manpower and equipment from North Vietnam. The maintenance of area security thus became a frustrating task, for no matter how dense our outpost system or how well motivate our troops were, the enemy could always find loopholes to penetrate and

weaknesses to exploit. Ups and downs in village security were an inevitable reality we always had to face…

What was supposed to have changed such that revisionists see the attitudes of villagers becoming favourable (rather than outwardly acquiescent) towards inquisitive US/GVN forces? The customary story is that, after many corruption-riddled fits and starts, authentic land reform did kick into gear and that, once enough property was handed over, the surly peasants transformed into prosperous market-oriented individualists (as Irish peasants had done under less combative conditions in the early twentieth century). Counterinsurgency policies at the same time, however, resulted in less land. As a military map-maker, Ngo Vinh Long over 1959-1963 visited "virtually every hamlet and village in the country." He saw how defoliation since 1961 drove peasants into squalid government camps, where they suffered starvation, illnesses and a catalogue of birth deformities. Long quotes a Japan Science Council investigator who said that by 1967 about half the arable soil had been poisoned by aerial spraying.

The few land reform specialists independent of the Southern authorities observed "a class-oriented program" heartily at work, and surmised that "no amount of wishful or ideological thinking could turn Diem, Kah, Ky or Thieu into champions of the laboring poor." The fond hope at the glittering Palace in Saigon was that one and a half hectares would suffice to create a loyal "middle" peasant out of an aggrieved tenant. Yet the evidence indicates instead that these middle peasants were more likely to yield NLF recruits since they had the surplus resources and the time and ability to participate. There was no "steady erosion" of communist or community ties on the part of these wealthier peasants, who were none too many anyhow.

The two ARVN generals confess that:

> during this period of hot war, therefore, village elections were only valid to the extent that they provided rural areas with a coating of democratic veneer, other than that they often served no useful purpose as far as the people were concerned. That elected village officials were compelled to undergo training and indoctrination at Vung Tau often caused concern and even suspicion among some of our people about the democratic system. However, this training and indoctrination were necessary if we wanted them to truly serve the people.

Indeed. That's the export brew of US democracy. General William DePuy nevertheless lamented that it "is difficult for this democracy of ours to deal with the political dimensions of insurgency," the "arbitrary and often undemocratic controls required" do not "go down well back here at home."

In 1971 the GVN claimed it was in "firm control" of hamlet security, saying that 85.13 percent of hamlets were entirely or relatively secure." A tiresome, impressive statistic. "These results were obtained at a time when VCI activities were at their lowest level and when Communist main and local forces were avoiding engagement in preparation for their next big push," allowed a spoilsport ARVN ranking officer. "The security attained was not a guarantee that it would be immune to enemy spoiling actions and that the trend was irreversible. Pacification setbacks could occur anytime the enemy chooses to strike."

Any imputed gains achieved through accelerated pacification were illusory or temporary. Underlying grievances were never intended to be addressed—not at the risk of undermining the local coalition forming an American-backed government. Grievances are given a brisk dismissive treatment in the *Manual* where "perceived injustices" are treated as ridiculous ruses dreamed up by neurotic insurgents. While the grievances don't matter, the impressionable people doing something about them do matter—which is a familiar stance for nervous authoritarian states to take. A self-servingly witless census-taking attitude meant that sheer opinions were taken at face value. Long points out that, for people eking out existences under a cruel regime and foreign occupation, the questions, "Do you believe the people should be masters?" and "Do you believe in democracy?" were understood as more resonant of the NLF and the North than of Saigon, but were coded to favour the latter.

"Humiliation was much on the minds of those involved in the making of American policy for Vietnam during the Spring and Summer of 1965," *The Pentagon Papers* attest. "The word, or phrases meaning the same thing, appears in countless memoranda." John McNaughton, assistant Secretary of Defense, said, "The present US objective in Vietnam is to avoid humiliation" and to do so inside an "escalating military stalemate." So far as the insurgents were concerned, when NLF casualties got too high… they just backed off and waited." The NLF, even when nursing its considerable wounds, held the initiative at all times. *The Pentagon Papers* also disclose a post-Tet System

Analysis finding that while "we have raised the price to NVN of aggression and support of the VC, it shows no lack of capability or will to match each new US escalation. Our strategy of attrition has not worked." Not to put too fine a point on it:

> Despite massive influx of 500 thousand US troops, 1.2 million tons a bombs a year, 400 thousand attack sorties per years, 200 thousand enemy KIA in three years, 20,000 US KIA, etc. our control of the countryside and defense of the urban areas is essentially at pre-August 1965 levels. We have achieved stalemate at a high commitment. A new strategy must be sought.

# VII. After Tet

Counterinsurgency was the adamant US answer to the wrong question about the nature of the conflict. The 1968 Tet offensive, Elliot finds, was as much a popular uprising as anything else; David Hunt calls it "the greatest of the peasant revolts." All "revisionists" argue that Tet was a great boon for the US/GVN. A sacred cliché today is that Tet was a political victory but a military defeat, which is a myopic and ultimately unimportant distinction. The insurgent forces sustained heavy losses but experienced little wavering of support. The US high command's assessment was that the insurgents easily regained the countryside as US and SVN troops were diverted to defend or recapture the assaulted cities. They acknowledged, internally, that most of the cities were none too secure either.

Further, the official statistics don't bother to offset NLF losses against hordes of prisoners freed from custody, who replenished the insurgency ranks. Despite the "accelerated pacification" phase afterward, it remained possible for the NLF and NVA to continue to launch equally devastating but not so highly publicized offensives after Tet. Generals Westmoreland and Wheeler both acknowledged, well out of media earshot, that Tet was no victory. In subsequent actions, such as "Mini-Tet" in April, Willbanks writes, "the Communist forces had clearly demonstrated that they had not been destroyed during the earlier Tet fighting."

The *Manual* nonetheless claims that by 1970 93 percent of rural South Vietnamese—those remaining after forced mass migrations to cities and camps—reside in "relatively secure villages" and that therefore the insurgency had been "uprooted." Yet Hunt found, contrary to rah-rah reports, that "US/GVN sweeps and mass killings seem to have pushed fence-sitters over the edge" so that many more young people were volunteering for the NLF. Those who didn't were being forced into the South Vietnamese military. Blaufarb argues that the real crime of Phoenix was "ineffectiveness, indiscriminateness, and, in some areas at least, the violation of the local norms to the extent that it appeared to the villagers to be a threat to them in the peaceful performance of their daily business." His view is that the American analysts involved "erred in not appreciating the extent to which the pathology of Vietnamese society would distort an apparently sound concept." How could they? It was this very "pathology" that the US/GVN troops, at great cost, were defending.

The blunt objective in My Tho province was "to destroy rather than 'pacify' the rural communities."

The bombing, pillaging, refugee flight, the GVN and NLF drafts, cadres killed, and cumulative hardships all led to an NLF retreat. Even so, the six villages studied in one Hamlet Evaluation Study remained "nearly completely controlled by the revolution as much in January 1968 as a year before." This unexpected result, for rational choice analysts, can be comprehended only in the terms of a game of gang warfare, a sort of *West Side Story* writ global where all rival forces are treated as symmetrical and as equally legitimate or illegitimate, which is coincidentally a depiction most amenable to application of formal modelling.

This stilted caricature must characterize the way that insurgents behave and think because the method of analysis demands it. The analysts, after all, don't work for the insurgents. There is no space for the abstract notions of nationalism or solidarity or social justice, only for self-regarding mafias who compete to compel obedience. This loyalty for the sake of gain cannot explain why the NLF was far more successful than the US/GVN, despite taking unbelievable punishment for so long. For if strict rational choice criteria informed the NLF's operating code, the Southern insurgency would have been extinguished in quick order. By the same token, had the Provisional IRA always acted as irrationally as they did in mass market movies like *The Crying Game* or *Patriot Games* the organization would have been wiped out in a week flat.

An ironclad rule of real counterinsurgency is that "carrot and stick," at the first sign of sustained resistance, becomes all stick. "We're going to beat the communists at their own game, use their methods, cut off their cocks, cut up their women and children, if that's what it takes, until we break the communist hold over these people," an indignant CIA official told a journalist in 1967. "*We can stand it.*" In Vietnam disembedded and disabused press members, such as the late David Halberstam and Peter Arnett, already had watched the vaunted Strategic Hamlet Program disintegrate before their very eyes, despite many "happy talk" briefings to the contrary.

The military's tradition of "doctoring" its reports goes back at least as far as the RAF's use of chemical weapons and gas upon recalcitrant Middle East villages in the 1920s, through the Nixon administration's secret bombing of Cambodia and Laos to initial denials of use of phosphorous bombs or napalm in Iraq today. As Henry Cabot Lodge advised Robert McNamara: "If you think these people are going to tell you or say in front of [General] Harkin what they really think unless it is what Harkin thinks, you just don't know the army." ("Two plus two always makes four. But first someone has to decide that two is actually two," observed George Allen, veteran CIA and defense analyst.) Some things never change, and do not require exotic terms like repetition compulsion to explain why.

Over 1970-1972 government agencies were divided in their appraisals on the effectiveness of pacification, depending to a large extent on whether they understood the Vietnamese conception of protracted war. In stark contrast to a "conventional warrior mentality," former central committee member Truong Nhu Tang in his *Viet Cong Memoir* contends that for the NLF and NVA:

> every military clash, every demonstration, every propaganda appeal was seen as a part of an intelligible whole: each had consequences far beyond its

immediate apparent result. It was a framework that allowed us to view battle as a psychological event and to undertake negotiations in order to strengthen the military posture. The Americans seemed never to appreciate fully this strategic perspective... It was after all a traditional Vietnamese approach to warfare, a technique refined over centuries of confrontation with invaders more powerful than ourselves.

The vaunted gains in the South Vietnamese countryside through accelerated pacification after November 1968 were far more ambiguous a phenomenon to interpret than anyone in uniform cared to admit. A MACV estimate said that total VC strength fell from 189 to 120 thousand in the three years after Tet. Yet, even if one took their picture as gospel, the result was that the VC adapted so that their small-unit actions accelerated from 1,374 in 1968 to 2,400 by 1972. It no doubt beats brigade-strength actions, but hardly constituted proof of victory just around the corner.

Davidson cites a fall in attacks on US/GVN forces from 32,362 in 1968 to 27,790 in 1969 and then 23,760 in 1970 as evidence of declining resistance. A mere 23,760 recorded attacks in one year became something to cheer about. According to the office of the Assistant Secretary of Defense (Public Affairs), in 1972 4,405 people were assassinated while insurgents abducted 13,119 people. This was a higher toll than in 1971, but lower than in 1968, 1969 and 1970 in terms of assassination, though not in number of abductions. Was it now safe for uniformed personnel to walk the streets unarmed?

"Pacification in the broadest sense—to which the reform of the GVN and PVANF [was needed]—

would never occur, but its narrow victory... was a resounding success," General Philip P. Davidson said afterward, in a quietly devastating judgment. "While they changed at the village level, at upper levels they did not, and short of a respite of many years, could not change." Even if "victory" in the short term had been in the offing, by this time, as Chalmers Johnson told an interviewer in 1997: "many senior analysts were passionately opposed to President Johnson and Richard Nixon's policies, and after the *Pentagon Papers* had been made public many of the analysts were quietly exultant that their pessimistic estimates of whether the US could win the war were now in an official part of the public record."

In spite of all the diligent scholarly crusades to revise the history of pacification, it is clear that the Pentagon was pessimistic or at least seriously divided about the prospects for pacification in Iraq. General David Petraeus, Princeton PhD, was a minority figure in that respect before he took over command of forces in Iraq, telling an interviewer in December 2006: "Counterinsurgency operations are war at the graduate level, they're thinking man's warfare." Even without the courtesy of courageous leaks of *Pentagon Papers* proportions, the rationales for the Iraq intervention unravelled beforehand for all but the true believers who never cared about the extremely embarrassing absence of WMDs afterward. The best excuse anyone can come up with is that US forces must stay in Iraq to tamp down the very cyclonic forces they triggered by invading in the first place. Why no Nuremberg style trials for those who concocted the invasion and its flimsy justifications? One sign of madness is the belief that only one's own willpower or actions matter, not those of the other folks inhabiting the relevant milieu. It does serve, for a good many, to keep twinges of conscience at bay, so perhaps madness is not quite the word for what is going on here.

## VIII. The Future of a Delusion

> The flames were all around you. I mapped it all out
> and seventy, eighty percent of the villages were just
> dust—ashes and dust. But that was not the story.
> The story was still how we were going to help the
> South Vietnamese resist the attack from the North.
> In Vietnam I learned about the capacity of the
> human mind to build a model of experience that
> screens out even very dramatic and obvious realities.
> —*Jonathan Schell*

The ennobling interpretation of the Vietnam War,
which played a role of enabler for the hideous
imbroglio today in Iraq, extends to the realm of film-
making. A four part documentary series, *Long Way
Home Project*, was based on credulity-straining research
exemplified by the aforementioned quintet of books.
One recalls the Right's outcry and its riposte program

to PBS' doggedly middle-of-the-road 13-part Vietnam War series in the 1980s—a campaign led by Reed Irvine's richly misnamed Accuracy in Media organization. Where then, one might ask, was the Left's riposte to the PBS series or the broadcasted AIM response? Anything a hair to the left of AIM was assailed as left-wing, so for those nettlesome folks there's no need for any further inquiry.

Part Two of the *Long Way Home Project*, "How We Won the War," relied heavily on Sorley and Moyar to argue that by the Summer of 1970 the rebels in South Vietnam were defeated and that most of the countryside was in friendly hands. "I left Vietnam in January of 1969 but was unaware of this success until decades later," one enthusiast of the series marvels. No surprise. The series filmmakers lament that the "American elite" seemed "impervious" to this startling notion. They claim that within a year of finishing the final cut, the series was adopted by high schools in 14 states for history or social science classes. Teachers receive the 4 part series, a guide, and a CD with documents in American history at no extra charge.

Annette Hall, producer with husband Don of "Silent Victory," remarked:

> Like you, we felt it was worth the high personal cost to create a documentary that tells the truth about the Vietnam War since so many deliberate lies and distortions have been forced fed to impressionable young people by the left-wing intellectual fanatics in academia and the media... the truth will prevail, hopefully in time to prevent the leftist intellectuals from succeeding in their quest to destroy this country.

Really? As compared to the blithe way the righteous patriots of the Bush II administration industriously shredded the economic security, political liberties and social rights of the average American?

The *Project* is introduced by retired Desert Storm commander, General Norman Schwarzkopf. "The university media, of course, will not mention this effort, but with enterprising teachers and students all over the country showing these films the prevailing lies about Vietnam on campus, institutionalized to protect those who would not serve, are going to be exposed and discredited," former History professor Leonard Magruder states. "And it is imperative that they be discredited as they are being recycled on campus to attack the nation's war on terrorism and this could lead to another polarization and then defeat as happened in the case of Vietnam."

The last battle of "the Vietnam War will not be for the hearts and minds of Indochinese villagers," a pro-war writer intones, "but rather for the hearts and minds of future generations of American children." Darn right. In his 1991 memoir *In the Shadow of Vietnam* Marine veteran and poet Bill Ehrhardt, by way of stark contrast, recounts his response when earnestly asked by a classroom of high school students decades later if a treasonous antiwar movement had demoralized him while in combat:

> What had damaged my morale, I told them, was the discovery that the people we had been sent to defend did not want us there—and indeed, more often than not and with good reason—hated us; that we had been ordered by our government to win the hearts and minds of the people of Vietnam with nothing

but rifles and bombs and bullets and American arrogance; that what we were involved in had nothing to do with the cause of liberty and democracy and freedom for which I had enlisted in 1966 at the age of 17; that we were redcoats, not patriots, and that our national leaders had put us up to it; that we were killing and dying for something worse than nothing.

The pupils, Erhardt learned, had been taught that America lost the Vietnam War because dirty disloyal protesters undermined troop morale. (One notes a creepy resonance with what was taught in German schools about the cause of defeat in the First World War.) One may boldly hypothesize that the more that citizens imbibe such establishment beliefs, the easier life will be for unscrupulous leaders and for the hordes of their mainstream media stenographers. The carefully omitted variables are behaving themselves; the "data" are conforming. Still, "counter-elites," like this angry veteran, inhabit the public realm too and have their own sobering experiences to convey.

Public judgments about past foreign policy undeniably affected the American State in the form of the Vietnam Syndrome, constraining military adventures for which there formerly was carte blanche. The Bush II administration, on the basis of its incipient *fuherprinzip* (aka, the "imperial presidency"), defiantly opted to override the syndrome in order to accomplish its aim of US corporate control of Iraqi energy—and possibly because it gambled that it could sway US election outcomes too through propaganda, intimidation, and voting legerdemain.

Let us return to the almighty *Manual*, which purveys the intoxicating news that by early 1970 93 percent of South Vietnamese lived in "relatively secure villages—an increase of 20 percent from the Middle of 1968." Thrillingly, "pacification had largely uprooted the insurgency [and] forced the Communists to rely more heavily on infiltrating conventional forces." The immense pretense here is that this insurgency could be defeated quickly and for good, regardless of a passionate ongoing national independence struggle. The Northerners, remarkably, were the real intruders, not the Americans or, before them, the French:

> Leaders in the governments of both the RVN and the DRV came from all over Vietnam, not only from the region in which their capital resided. The Diem government, for example, contained many Catholics who had migrated from the North in 1954, and later Vice President Nguyen Cao Ky provided a highly visible "northern" presence in the Saigon government. More important, however, was the "southern" presence in the highest ranks of the DRV leadership. Le Duan, the First Secretary of the Central Committee of the Vietnamese Workers Party was born in Quang Tri, just south of the 17th parallel. Pham Van Dong, the Prime Minister of the DRV, was born in Quang Ngai. Pham Hung, a Vice-Premier of the DRV and member of the Political Bureau since the late 1950s, was from Ving Long, and Ton Duc Thang, who succeeded Ho Chi Minh as President of the DRV, was born in the Mekong Delta. Nguyen Chi Thanh, the DRV military commander in the South until his death in 1967, was also a southerner. Such biographical information led one author to conclude that "in terms of the birthplace of opposing leaders, it is evident that the Second Indochina War was more of a civil war than was America's war of 1860-1865.

The *Manual*, based on the scriptures of the rehabilitators, is the narrative they tell themselves. "COIN is
an intelligence-driven endeavor"—but only of the kind
the masters want to hear. Look no further than the infa-
mous pre-Tet underestimate of main and local NLF
forces. A claim to have reached the fabled "crossover
point" where enemy losses exceed replacement capacity
is the reason why the US Military late in 1967 preferred
figures of about 300,000, an underestimate of 120 to
200 thousand foes, achieved by dropping militia self-
defense (SD) forces from the Order of Battle.

Carver writes that the CIA wound up "acceding
to MACV" through a "disingenuous cooking of the
books." So the "concern was not an accurate count of
the enemy forces but concern over the press, intelligence has been politicized," Jake Blood concludes in
*Tet: Intelligence and the Public Perception of the War*.
Questions arose over the news-gathering practices of a
1982 CBS documentary on the subject but not about
the reality of the actual "uncounted enemy." Brigadier
General Davidson of MACV argued that the exclusion
of the SD forces was made because they were "militar-
ily insignificant" and that the American people might
not properly interpret their "combat capabilities."

Combat capability is a matter for narrowly military expertise to suss out. Of far greater concern to
anxious leaders was that the American people correctly
would grasp that they were facing the Vietnamese
people *en masse*, who opposed US presence in what was
really a protracted civil war. Neither the generals nor
the administration wanted the public to suspect that
Vietnam was a very different kind of war than the clean,
selfless and necessary one they were being told was
fought.

A senior South Asian civil servant I knew visited Saigon in 1959. The US build-up was in its early stages but big Yanks already were conspicuous in the sweltering city streets. One afternoon he teasingly asked a pretty bargirl if, because they were big spenders, she were pro-American. She startled him by breaking into tears. She explained that, like most city people, she had family in the villages and no one knew from one day to the next even then if relations had escaped strafing and shelling, courtesy of American "advisors." Harvard scholar Samuel Huntington, incidentally, was among those urging forced urbanization to wrench Vietnam "out of the phase in which a rural revolutionary development can hope to generate sufficient strength to come to power." As a US official remarked at a cocktail party, "Sam has lost the capacity to distinguish between urbanization and genocide."

Later, in 1966, a senor journalist colleague met an elegant young Vietnamese woman in Saigon who taught English at the university. When asked if it were possible to meet Viet Cong members, she bridled at the term, which the Southern regime used to disparage the resistance, and replied with teeth-gritted politeness, "What do you mean? Do you mean a member of the Vietnamese liberation army?" He nodded. "Then, yes. I am a member of the Viet Cong," she affirmed. "Everyone here is a Viet Cong. During the day I teach English and during nights I work for the liberation." Could the *Manual*, under any likely form of revision, ever confront or cope with these dismaying "background" facts about any insurgency?

Asked if she felt disheartened in grim wartime conditions, the teacher calmly responded that these were the only conditions she knew. Always war. She had been born during the Japanese occupation. She had seen the most vicious counter-insurgency programs come and go. The overall plight evokes the frequent jest among old Vietnam hands—including, allegedly, official land reform advocate Roy Prosterman—that the US much more cheaply could have bribed the peasantry to flock to the Saigon regime's side, or at least to pretend to. The US/GVN regime preferred to batter the peasantry into such pretenses though coercion.

What would it actually have meant to have "won" that war (and for how long would it have stayed won)? What conditions would have to prevail for "pacification" to have worked, at least in the demeanor of the sullen subjects of it? The US conducted the war as one of overwhelming technological lethality geared to "attrite" whoever got in the line of fire as fast as possible. For the NLF and Hanoi, it was instead a perpetual nationalist war, if need be, to eject all colonial holdovers. Against such resolve, the US rolled out "accelerated pacification," Vietnamization, more carpet bombings, and a "Clear and Hold" approach on the ground, which wasn't everything it wanted to appear to be.

The *Manual's* creed holds that, given time, counterinsurgents can and will crush the local populace into abject submission. Competent authorities round up designated rebels and terminate them, "with extreme prejudice." Everything afterward will be sweetness, of a sickly feigned sort, and light, lit by napalm and phosphorous. In their best-laid plans, overly prudent American policymakers, the revisionists carp, never had the slightest intention of demolishing North Vietnam—perhaps due to the distinct prospect of several million Chinese troops pouring down into the melee. All the "we can win" scenarios that get trotted out are equally far-fetched and question-begging.

Capturing the dilemma perfectly (but unaware of it) a gung-ho observer regrets "a bitter irony that while the U.S. did come to the immediate rescue of the [South Vietnam regime], by our own subsequent actions we were inadvertently condemning them to a long-term catastrophic defeat." Such sad accounts are accompanied by bilious disdain for spoilsports at home who unwisely exercised their right to protest and work to reverse a US policy riddled with hubris, ineptitude and ignorance—and blanketed by innumerable deceits. Theirs not to reason why; it's not in the job description. Reasoning why is a job for ordinary citizens, for whom these neo-militarists who call themselves revisionists display precious little respect.

In January 1998 I visited Vietnam, intending, among other things, to write about commemorations on the 30th anniversary of the turning-point Tet offensive. The story turned out to be that there was no story, no celebrations, no ceremonies of any kind. The lone reference to Tet I found was a fuzzy-screened TV parked on the steps of the Presidential Palace in the city formerly known as Saigon, which played a re-looping videotape of the 1968 attacks. I was later told that the Government, seeking investment and better trade relations with the US, wanted everything kept low-key. Celebrations might be an embarrassment. Here was the dire fate—the result of failed pacification, the worst possible outcome—for which so much blood was shed and so much treasure wasted for so long in vain to avert.

# IX. Counterinsurgency Blues

The *Manual* authors assume that counterinsurgents will be implacable implementers of policy, immune to second thoughts, or any thought at all. The self-styled "revisionists," however, bewail the poor discipline, low morale, racist fissures, and outright fragging afflicting the American military, especially during the Vietnamization phase of the war under Nixon. They believe the diagnosis is obvious. "There flourished a widely imitated popular culture," Sorley accuses, "that included its own music, recreational drug use, and renunciation of any notion of obligation to the larger society." One scratches one's head. Is there emblazoned upon the US flag a tied bundle of sticks, rather than stars and stripes? For consummate patriots, resisting a crazy, costly, needless war is the same as renouncing one's obligations to the larger society.

Sorley asserts that mass disciplinary breakdowns erupted only after the troops began to be withdrawn, which happens to coincide with the admission even by LBJ's "wise men" committee that the war, after Tet, was unwinnable. While the revisionists tirelessly trot out statistics of enemy losses, villages secured, areas cleared and held, VC defections, and HES percentages, there remained a neglected dimension of dissent and disaffection, as many soldiers mulled over their cannon-fodder status in a war they realized made no moral or strategic sense.

An ARVN General cites VC desertion totals reaching 159,000 by 1971, two thirds of them soldiers. The desertions were anointed a sure sign of the bankruptcy of the enemy's cause. Meanwhile, back in what today quasi-Teutonically is called the "Homeland," draft evaders and war resisters were far outpaced by deserters. During 1971 nearly a hundred thousand servicemen deserted, a rate of 142.2 for every 1,000 men on duty. Franklin notes:

> According to the Department of Defense, there were 503,926 "incidents of desertion" between July 1, 1966, and December 31, 1973. From 1963 through 1973 (a period almost half again as long), only 13,518 men were prosecuted for draft evasion or resistance. The admitted total of deserters still officially "at large" at the time was 28,661—six and half times the 4,400 draft evaders or resisters still "at large."

Vietnam correspondent Richard Boyle in *Flower of the Dragon* says that, after the bloody assaults in May 1969 on Hamburger Hill, the 101st airborne troopers put out an underground newspaper, with one issue carrying an "award of 10 grand for killing the officer who ordered the attack." The site in question had no strategic value and was "enshrined in GI folklore as Hamburger Hill, because of the 56 men killed and 420 wounded taking it. Despite several fragging attempts, Honeycutt escaped uninjured." Those embarrassing infractions were omitted from a 1987 Hollywood movie where soldiers condemn the "dirty hippie" protesters who were trying to bring them home alive, but who have no problem whatsoever with promotion-hunting "lifer" leaders. Something between insubordination and insurgency actually erupted in countless low-level ways within the ranks during what many ordinary soldiers understood was a surreally futile war.

Boyle and others chronicled the drug use, the racism eventuating in the Long Binh jail revolt in 1968, a venal culture of "lifers versus the rest" plus the chasm between rear echelon upper ranks and everyone else in what Ronald Reagan later deemed a "noble cause." Clearly not all the soldiers, sailors and airmen saw it that way. "I was sure there would have been open revolt by the troops in Vietnam," Boyle reckoned, "if not for one thing—each grunt knew he had only one year to do" which he had to weigh against a 5 year jail sentence. Among the South Vietnamese—those "Asian boys" whom LBJ promised not to send "American boys" to fight in their stead—there was a 20 percent desertion rate and, to encourage the others, two hundred thousand political prisoners suffered in horrid conditions in the South.

After Tet, the simmering discontent intensified and spawned many forms of foot-dragging resistance among the troops up to and including violent ones. At least 800 to 1,000 fragging attempts occurred. Joel Geier notes:

> The army reported 126 fraggings in 1969, 271 in 1970 and 333 in 1971, when they stopped keeping count. …Some military estimates are that fraggings occurred at five times the official rate, while officers of the Judge Advocate General Corps believed that only 10 percent of fraggings were reported. These figures do not include officers who were shot in the back by their men and listed as wounded or killed in action.

The "soldier's revolt was kept under wraps at the time" and long afterward. The 2005 documentary *Sir, No Sir—The GI Revolt* is one of the few works disinterring this phenomenon. The documentary *Winter Soldier* in 1972 was another. Acknowledging the reality of internal military dissent would spoil the febrile John Wayne image that conservatives ritually invoke, depicting troops as ever willing to do what they were told to do. A small minority, 2.5 million men (about 10 percent of the total eligible for the draft), actually were dispatched to Vietnam. Many of them were goggle-eyed at the lavish corruption they encountered. The Viet Cong garnered a great deal of their supplies "from the United States via the underground routes of the black market: kerosene, sheet metal, oil, gasoline engines, claymore mines, hand grenades, rifles, bags of cement," which were publicly sold at open, outdoor black markets.

Tet demonstrated, Geier adds, that the NLF had very wide support—"millions knew of and collaborated with the NLF entry into the cities and no one warned the Americans." By 1971 a quarter of the armed forces was absent without leave, deserted or was imprisoned. Countless others had received "Ho Chi Minh discharges" for being disruptive and troublemaking. The army recorded 68 such mutinies that year. By 1970, in the 1st Air Cavalry Division alone, there were 35 acts of combat refusal.

The form this "peace from below" took became so extensive that "search and evade (meaning tacit avoidance of combat by units in the field) became widespread. Some officers joined, or led their men, in the unofficial cease-fire from below. A U.S. army colonel claimed:

> I had influence over an entire province. I put my men to work helping with the harvest. They put up buildings. Once the NVA understood what I was doing, they eased up. I'm talking to you about a de facto truce, you understand. The war stopped in most of the province. It's the kind of history that doesn't get recorded. Few people even know it happened, and no one will ever admit that it happened.

## X. Touchy-Feely Domination

The *Manual*'s "hearts and minds" dimension is PR gossamer, set to blow away at the first gust of resistance. Beneath the perfunctory sensitive verbiage is a remorseless *Robocop* perspective (with none of the ironic fun that the original movie had with the moronic concept). Culture, says the *Manual*, is "a web of meaning." But what does this truism mean when you, as a military force, confront an enemy whose core beliefs, based on hard experience, differ profoundly from your own? Clearly, scholars kitted out in military gear obediently will paint by the numbers that someone else has determined for them.

What the *Manual* is hunting for is not meaning but rather the identities of those who hold power in the strange turf, and then to figure out either how to use them or target them. The quest boils down to scraping up "intelligence on the location and identity of the insurgent enemy derived from a supportive population"—if possible. The *Manual* speaks only of "perceived" injustices, "which include economic disenfranchisement, exploitative economic arrangements, and significant income disparities." Why is it that these harmful things—eminently measurable, by the way—become degraded in a snap of a policy analyst's fingers to mere matters of perception?

Has the military gone deliriously post-modern? Indeed it has if your ambition is to shape perceptions at home about what you are doing abroad. Here is the unbridled military managerial mentality at work, as it was in the celebrated case of *faux* heroine Jessica Lynch in Iraq (who became truly heroic when exposing official lies told about herself) and in the covered-up "friendly fire" killing in Afghanistan of former NFL star Pat Tillman, whose parents report that he had deep misgivings about the mission. The post-9/11 US news media—with honorable exceptions that can be counted on the fingers of one hand—abandoned any remaining investigative impulses to fall into line with Dubya's disinformation campaign, a story deserving a pamphlet all its own in this series.

Why the media conforms is exemplified in star journalists who can rely on *chutzpah* and eye-blink memories to pretend they were always on the side of the angels. In Baghdad in January 2003, for example, while traveling with an "academics for peace" delegation I encountered the *Washington Post*'s bureau chief Rajiv Chandrasekaran who was sniffing around for an easy derogatory story. The "party line" at the *Post* was to echo the able administration. He duly filed a report hinting that we and other antiwar activists were collaborators with Saddam. A few years later, moist fickle finger in the wind, he scribbled an anti-war bestseller *Imperial Life in the Emerald City* on outrageous US activities in the Green Zone. It is not what one would call with a straight face doing penance. These cautious and crafty shape-shifters never seem to lose. Why then should media people ever take any risks?

Coming back to the *Manual*, the question whether grievances are valid is a big one that it must take a pass on. For if grievances turn out to be valid, why dispatch hordes of trained killers to punish people already suffering under such arrangements? The *Manual*, implausibly, abjures "physically destroying the unseen opponent embedded in the general population." If it really did, there would be no reason for pacification. A pious statement that US forces "must assume more risk" is beyond risible since that is the last thing one reasonably can hope they will do. "Human nature is a funny thing," a South Armagh pub-keeper, sympathetic to Irish Republicanism, told me during the height of the "troubles." What he meant was that it was not at all strange that the British soldiers he witnessed under threat over decades always looked after themselves first, and at whatever cost to others.

To expect otherwise of human beings is itself dangerously disingenuous. US forces in Iraq and Afghanistan are renowned for shooting up civilian cars that venture within shouting distance of their own vehicle, or which move a tad too fast toward checkpoints. Even Iraqi Prime Minister Nouri al-Maliki complained that US forces showed "no respect for citizens, smashing civilian cars and killing on a suspicion or a hunch." In Afghanistan, according to UN figures in 2007, civilian deaths over the first 6 months resulting from US,

*US Marines clear an abandoned house during a weapons sweep across the Thar Thar Lake area in Iraq, June 2005.*

NATO and Afghan government action outnumbered those caused by the Taliban. In March that year a suicide bomber struck a Marine convoy near Jalalabad, killing one serviceman: As pedestrians scattered in the resulting confusion and chaos, other marines opened fire as their convoy sped away, shooting at vehicles and pedestrians over the course of some 10 miles, according to the Afghanistan Independent Human Rights Commission. They left at least 12 civilians dead in their wake and injured dozens more. "They opened fire on everybody," one wounded bystander told a reporter, "the ones inside the vehicles and the ones on foot... the Afghan human rights commission have already concluded that the American convoy was not fired upon after the suicide attack," reported the *Washington Post* (18 November, 2007.) The carnage continues. In September 2009 NATO air strikes on 2 captured gas trucks wound up killing dozens of civilians.

The more's the pity because the *Manual* refreshingly recognizes that the "key to success in counterinsurgency is protecting the population" and that "needlessly harming the local people can harm the counterinsurgent too because any action is counterproductive that causes "collateral damage" and "leads to recruitment of fifty new insurgents." That is surely good policy even if it is stated in off-puttingly pragmatic terms. One must infer that if the authors surmised that they could inflict needless harm with impunity and to the benefit of their own mission, they would feel perfectly free to do so. That's the cruel underlying realist logic at play; the crass matter-of-fact Athenians still taunt the underdog Melians.

The *Manual* conflates insurgency with terrorism. Another premise, so far as the distribution of power is concerned, is that whatever is, is right. So counterinsurgency "favors peace and justice" while insincere insurgents only "claimed to be fighting the injustice of monarchy, imperialism and repression." A *Manual* preface obligatorily mentions "profound questions about which wars the US should fight" while bemoaning that "Iraq has bred a familiar cynicism that risks disengaging Americans from the government and America from the world." Cynicism effectively is defined here as any negative assessment of government versions of reality. Cynicism is not earned by encounters with past state misbehavior. By the *Manual*'s terms, the only stance that is not cynical is cheerful acceptance of the terms of the debate as laid down by the superiors of those who authored the *Manual*, who one at times suspects do not cast reflections, let alone indulge in them.

So trembling villagers in Colombia today are unjustifiably cynical to believe that government and allied paramilitary forces (aka death squads) have anything but their best interests at heart. My Lai survivors are cynical to imagine that the atrocities there were anything but the fault of one epically inept lieutenant—rather than of the impassive meat grinder apparatus of pacification. Massacre survivors in El Salvador too ought to be ashamed of fearing the well-intentioned Atlacatl Division. Some 40 thousand people were killed there over 1981-83 alone during pacification sweeps. All guerrillas.

Sound familiar? In fact, a Land to the Tiller program in El Salvador was viewed frankly by planners as "a PR exercise." The influence of the landlords was reckoned to be too great to confront. The Americans saw this proposed paper reform as "a political imperative to help prevent political collapse, strike a bow to the left, and help prevent radicalization of the rural population," who nefariously leaned to the FMLN. Smith found that the program was "poorly planned, weakly managed, subverted by El Salvador's right wing, and ultimately aimed more to change perception about land inequality then equality itself." Participating in government reform afforded no protection either. In December 1980, John Pilger wrote:

> [Jose] Viera, President of the El Salvador Land Reform Institute and a former campesino, accused the latest junta of undermining attempts at land reform after he discovered that wealthy land owners were being paid double the true value of their properties and that the colonels in the junta were taking their cut, leaving the peasants with nothing. "We were tricked," Viera announced, "and [the colonels] are shooting our people like dogs." On 3 January

1981, while having coffee at the Sheraton Hotel; with two officials of USAID, he was hit by thirty bullets... [The two officials also were killed.]

El Salvador too was graced with "strategic hamlets" and other retreaded Vietnam devices. The scarred experts wanted to get it right that time too. Wood adds: "Under the cover of the state of siege (declared the day after the land reforms were announced.), and the turmoil occasioned by the expropriation of properties, violence escalated as government forces targeted *campesino* activists." Phase II of the reform, affecting 150-500 hectare estates, was never implemented. So much for the civic dimension.

The *Manual* ignores, or edits, insurgency experiences that readers might not want to counter. American rebels in the mid-1770s fit the *Manual's* criteria for a "resistance movement," defined "as indigenous elements seeking to expel or overthrow what they perceive to be a foreign or occupation government." Should a deft application of British force have kept America snug inside the benevolent empire? The ultimate message is that "lessons learned" elsewhere are supposed to be able to help pacify Iraq or Afghanistan. This is missionspeak: a garbled one-way logic brooking no thought outside its frontiers.

The logic leads willy-nilly into infernal regions. Perhaps the French resistance, such as it was, ought to be admonished for defying the occupation. The fascists, French and German, were lawful authorities. For *Manual* writers, that legal requirement clearly is all they need or want to know. In the 20th century four times as many people (170 million) were murdered by lawful state-sponsored violence as were killed during all wars and civil wars. Perhaps the first order of enlightened business for humanity is a bonfire of the *Manuals*.

## XI. How Learning Curves

The *Manual* assumes that established governments enjoy wide legitimacy, and only need modest aid to bolster them against malcontents and meddlers. A state that cannot stand up to its own stomped-on population is not thinkable in the neat universe our counterinsurgency specialists inhabit. The soldiers doing this required reading do not get to pick those insurgencies they believe are worth fighting. While the *Manual* exhibits a touching faith in the supportiveness of populations in foreign countries where the US lends a hand, it is mighty suspicious of the folks back home. Regarding the most controversial war the US ever fought, the *Manual* resorts to stab-in-the-back theory, as the enemy after Tet is portrayed as having shifting "from defeating US forces in Vietnam to weakening US will at home, and succeeded. Is there another

*Manual*—classified—for dispensing propaganda on the home front?

It is perhaps worth pondering, what is so successful about the successful counterinsurgency cases? The aforementioned "Malayan emergency" outlasted national independence (1957) by three years. In Kenya during the Mau Mau insurgency of the 1950s the Kikuyu lost eleven thousand "killed in action" versus less than a hundred dead Europeans. Of one and a half million Kikuyu, 30 thousand were imprisoned and 80 thousand routed into foul detention camps. The "strategic hamlets" program uprooted over one million Kenyans between 1952-55, and there was a population loss somewhere between 130 thousand and 300 thousand. Some remedial measures were taken to deeply justified grievances. The insurgency was quelled. Is Kenya then still a member in good standing of the British empire? Jomo Kenyatta became the first President of an independent Kenya in 1963. That went well.

In Northern Ireland, a ceasefire was agreed to in 1994, faltered, was renewed in 1996 and has held ever since. The triumph that counterinsurgency fans crow about only makes sense if the IRA had started the fray, which it most certainly didn't. A constitutional movement to win "equal rights for British citizens" arose among Catholic communities in the North in the 1960s and was thwarted by police-supported mobs. Violence engendered escalating violence. The *Manual*'s authors preposterously portray the heavily armed loyalists militias as "arising in reaction" to the IRA. This account mangles the actual sequence of events, but once armed resistance gets under way, the crude rule is to ignore everything except the fact of the insurgency.

One can't really blame a soldier for doing so, but the whole point of the *Manual* is to pretend that it is an exercise in pure reason. So, despite hindsight of 40 years, the *Manual* advises that if government cannot provide protection, people may organize armed militias to provide that essential service. And that is exactly how and why the dormant IRA revived in the late 1960s, to provide the essential service of protecting the Catholic community from the local sectarian police force and the armed militias. In 1969 the British Army arrived, almost fatally compromised, "in aid of the civil power," that is to say, in aid of a government whose misrule was the issue to begin with.

There are no nicer words than bigotry or stupidity to describe the thoroughly skewed manner in which the *Manual* writers portray this conflict. Do they not know of RUC-UDR-intelligence links that stoked death squad murders in the 6 (of a total of 9) counties of Ulster during a dirty war? British authorities, one

*An IRA mural in Belfast depicting the hunger strikes of 1981.*

has to conclude, probably behaved marginally better than the *Manual* writers would have in their places. The fraught peace process in the North over the 1990s surely is not a phenomenon that the *Manual* writers could have foreseen, allowed or desired. If Northern Ireland (or Vietnam) is to be a sterling example of the sophistication these counterinsurgency researchers wield, then nothing about the *Manual* is remotely trustworthy. One also doubts that the higher ranks and intelligence services actually believe this guff anyway, which is intended to sooth credulous civilians, but one always could be wrong.

Banished from the analytical equation are centuries of settler domination, sectarian discrimination, and police state rule in a neo-colonial statelet. The first bombs of the 1960s "troubles" were planted by Protestant terrorist groups so as to blame the IRA, who recently had peddled their arms to the Welsh and veered into ameliorative leftwing constitutional politics. "The IRA's response was reactive," as veteran journalist Ed Moloney, among innumerable experts, notes, "not remounting a war for reunification at first." The Catholic community lived in oppressive straits in the 6 counties, finally reacted, and in the course of doing so constitutionally became the "problem," instead of the problem being defined foremost as the Orange mini-state's discriminatory mechanisms.

Over ensuing decades, a mixture of carrot and stick indeed came into play as the British tried to build up a Catholic middle class of moderates while simultaneously criminalizing the largely working class insurgent nationalists, who became increasingly leftist as the crisis wore on. "In some ways," John Darby sums up, "the people who have benefited the most from public subsidy are Northern Ireland's middle class, not the poor." Catholics in Northern Ireland still experience discrimination so that "even when educational and practical qualifications are held constant, very large differences remain between Protestants and Catholic unemployment rates." Despite introducing the "most vigorous, if not perfect, affirmative action programme in the European Union," the Standing Advisory Commission on Human Rights there notes that although measures succeeded in diminishing discrimination in public services (most notably excepting the 93 percent Protestant Royal Ulster Constabulary). Catholics, after 30 years of ameliorative measures, still endure twice the unemployment of Protestants.

The British army, local police, and intelligence services neither endeared nor legitimate themselves to the Catholic population. The notion that the IRA alone was forced to the negotiating table is propaganda for the consumption of the mainland British home crowd. It was a two-way street, as both sides gave ground on their original positions in response to the wear and tear of the conflict. In 1978 the leaked British Army Glover Report shattered the illusion that the IRA were mere thugs and criminals. The IRA were smart, disciplined and ideologically motivated and capable of waging war indefinitely. For rational choice mavens, however, the IRA and its splinters are exactly like every other compulsorily nondescript rebel army.

Propaganda, which is what the *Manual*'s account patently is, is self-destructive since what customarily occurs is a feeding of official news to journalists whose words in print the government eventually believes itself. The ceasefire of 1994 and of 1996 owed little to security force behavior. Given the pathetic mis-

or disinformed portrayal of other guerrilla conflicts, one cannot be heartened by the opening lines of the *Manual* advising that "the better learning organization usually wins." Learning is curved, or curbed, according to the organizational needs of the moment. Ah, but a good leader, according to the *Manual*, can accomplish a poorly conceived, and even idiotic, mission. There always seems to be one for every such job.

Exceptions do exist. In May 1966 during the Vietnam escalation, former Marine Corps four star General David Shoup contrarily expressed the heretical lesson that "if we had, and would, keep our dirty, bloody, dollar-crooked fingers out of the business of these nations so full of depressed, exploited people, they will arrive at a solution of their own. That they design and want. That they fight and work for... and not the American style, which they don't want. Not one crammed down their throats by the Americans." Shoup was exercising the kind of leadership the *Manual* prefers to discourage.

## XII. Iraq and Afghan Follies

The *Manual* counsels that "restoring basic services should be regarded as a promise that US troops should avoid making, or even trying to do something about." So US troops in charge of a wracked and ruined country are off the hook for repairing or even running it. The fault is not a disinclination to get vital services up and running again, but rather in taking them on as tasks. No one will otherwise notice your irresponsibility. This is malevolent bureaucratese—the niggling myopic legalese of the conquerors, of an elite with enough insulation, enough power, to be protected from the consequences of their own actions—and who to some degree believe they can control those consequences too.

General Petraeus, who in 2008 took charge of the US Central Command overseeing all military operations abroad, offered a 14-point program for conducting counterinsurgency war in Iraq. One is especially struck by two formulations. The first is that "America's overwhelming conventional military superiority makes it unlikely that future enemies will confront us head on. Rather, they will attack us asymmetrically, avoiding our strengths..." So the military is treating asymmetrical tactics as if they were conducted by a unitary enemy that would prefer a head-on confrontation if at all possible, that wants to conquer the United States, if not the world. Automatic threat-inflation is implicit in Petraeus' formulation. The Cold War, with its innumerable proxy fights on the periphery, is back, if perhaps under an exotic new veil. Second, Petraeus advises that "in a situation like Iraq, the liberating force must act quickly, because every Army of liberation has a half-life beyond which it turns into an Army of occupation." True, but both half-lives expired several years ago. The US troops will never be seen by anyone not on its payroll as anything but dangerous and deeply resented occupiers.

This low-key crusade to rehabilitate pacification desperately, if slowly, has been under way ever since the Vietnam War ended. Defense Secretary Robert Gates too blandly argues that the Vietnam War was winnable. One is struck by how invested soldiers and strategists are in retaining this malfunctioning tool in their kit. Pacification is an enabler, an enabler of the mass firepower option. Firepower, in turn, enables cluelessness to take charge. An American General actually advises that the Iraqi government embarks "on its own neighborhood watch effort, encouraging the population to invest in its own security." Neighborhood watch? No neighborhoods anywhere on earth are watched so carefully by so many interested parties.

"Surely the rank and file of the people oppose the terrorist acts that are disrupting normal life in their cities and towns and will respond to an effort to organize themselves to provide security, especially for their children," the General, who is dead certain we are the good guys, opines. "It would be pleasing to learn in a couple of years that neighborhood watch groups have become Iraqi ruff-puffs and have taken over the local security role throughout the country." Doesn't every household already own an obligatory AK-47? Another general, William Buykin, who in 2003 was responsible for putting together a "new group of elite troops" called Task Force 121 for the Pentagon, the year before told a church congregation in Oregon that US is at war with "Satan who wants to destroy us." Call a shrink? No, on second thought, an exorcist is cheaper; that is, unless Blackwater is supplying the service.

In Iraq the psychic mechanisms in play are secondary to the material interests pursued by the neocon visionaries in the White House (who "make reality") but nonetheless are important in sustaining their grandiose grand strategy. Could the sorely expensive Iraqi occupation, under any imaginable circumstances, have succeeded? The quaint delusion is widespread, especially among liberal pundits, that George W. Bush might have avoided an intractable insurgency if only he had made a shrewder move here or there.

Maybe if the Iraqi Army had been kept intact, things would have worked out. Maybe if the Saddam loyalists had been kept behind their desks or in uniform, things would have worked out. Maybe if the impulsive US had waited to amass a military force twice its size (as many military commanders urged) before invading, things would have worked. Maybe if honest contractors had gotten electricity and water running again, things would have worked out. Maybe if the US rulers wouldn't privatize everything in sight to sell it off to cronies, things would work out.

So goes the mournful litany—with verses added daily. Presumably, then, if all the conditions above were met, Iraqis of all stripes would sit perfectly still while the West siphoned their resources. (The British military's conceit that they possessed a magic formula for conducting a "decent" occupation finally crumbled too.) The Coalition Provisional Authority long ago established a "parallel government structure of Commissioners and Inspectors-General... who, elections notwithstanding, will control Iraq's chief ministries." But one might concede that it all might have worked out if a US government of a radically different character had invaded—except that such a government would have read intelligence data honestly and therefore opted not to invade. The *Manual*, in any case, is more important for domestic consumers—a PR move on the propaganda chessboard—than for anything it portends abroad.

The ballyhooed withdrawal of US troops in Iraq is mostly a mirage. Obama began his administration by continuing Bush's intended version of Vietnamization, changing the color of the corpses of the soldiers, but keeping an ample military presence there to control Iraqi oil reserves. That's no way to dispel distrust of US motives in the Middle East. Iraq, like Vietnam during McNamara's heyday, now threatens to become a Whiz kid's war, where glib counterinsurgency experts apply violent force in what they imagine are precise doses to persuade a stubborn and ill-understood enemy to give up. It took McNamara decades to admit that US foreign policy in Southeast Asia was hopelessly and recklessly wrong.

The US under Obama, at least in his first year, pathetically is poised to replay the same pointless gory idiocies in Afghanistan. Sending in gung-ho military forces that can't seem to tell the difference between a guerrilla group and a wedding party is no boon to

*Col. Kevin Wilkerson, Commander 2nd Brigade, briefs US President George W. Bush on the Browning heavy machine gun, Fort Drum, NY.*

regional peace. The overpouring of violence into Pakistan's Western regions hardly testifies in favor of the wisdom of intrusive US policies. Observing NATO strategy, former Pentagon analyst Franklin Spinney warns:

> NATO strategists would also do well to remember how the "strategists" in [Vietnam and in the Soviet/Afghan war] insensibly became obsessed with bombing lines of communication. In the end, frustration, coupled with the insensible seduction of firepower and conventional dogma, led to attrition and destruction becoming ends in themselves...

No happy outcome lies on the receding horizon.

Obama seems to have worked out a tacit deal with the military-industrial complex to reduce troops in Iraq in exchange for ratcheting up Afghan hostilities to justify our astronomic military spending levels. "Defense-related spending for fiscal 2008 will exceed $1 trillion for the first time in history," Chalmers Johnson observes, "and one sees nary a question or complaint about it in the mainstream media." In November the national debt had breached $9 trillion, up from 5.7 trillion when Bush slipped into office in 2001. "This huge debt can be largely explained by our defense expenditures in comparison with the rest of the world." Arms spending should be the first place one looks when examining why there is no money for social needs at home or development schemes abroad Defense spending has doubled since the mid-1990s. Lockheed Martin, Northrop Grumman, Boeing, Raytheon are doing great, though military expenditures no longer come close to providing the stimulus the economy needs to come to former employment levels. Who needs to wage a risky hair-trigger cold war when a counterinsurgency doctrine aimed mostly at illiterate, ill-armed but smart tribesman will do the trick?

# Conclusion: A Meditation on
# *The Quiet American*

Stereotypes can be valuable if they are treated as background caricatures against which to cast the silhouettes of the real people they misportray. According to cherished stereotypes, Americans overseas dress badly, talk loudly, walk stiffly, speak languages clumsily, and regard everything they see as a primitive version of American goods or manners. Roving Yanks were described in the 19th century by one of their own number, Mark Twain, as "innocents abroad," but not, as the fiercely anti-imperialist Twain knew all too well, when it came to grabbing power or wealth. Innocence and greed make for a strange, if highly combustible, mixture.

When loot is at stake the stereotypes shift into dark devious images more befitting a superpower, whose elites are pleased to profit from economic activities on foreign soil without the unpleasant need to occupy any of it. American ties to loathsome leaders abroad (Somoza, Diem, Suharto, the Shah, etc.) for mutual gain are there for anyone who bothers to have a look. This low-key buccaneering approach is not peculiarly American, it is what major powers always get up to whenever they can get away with it.

In the 1950s novelist Graham Greene, just back from a stint in Indochina, published a slim but potent work of fiction, *The Quiet American*. This novel rightly came to be acclaimed, especially in the aftermath of US intervention in Southeast Asia, as a prophetic master-piece about the perils of bellicose idealism. With the supremely jaundiced eye of the sly British spy he once (or still) was, Greene skewered what he foresaw as the hopeless enterprise that American true believers launched after Dien Bien Phu in order to "save" Vietnam—but for whom?

As seen through the eyes of an opiated English journalist, Greene's title character Alden Pyle is a naïve covert operative who is serenely incapable of seeing that his government acts out of anything but altruism. Whatever the US foreign policy officials decree must be an unalloyed good for everyone. Pyle, when one steps back a bit, is a hollow, unpersuasive character, an over-grown boy scout meddling in complex struggles with clueless homicidal panache. His "innocence is a disease," Greene wrote. Pyle sauntered along "like a leper without a bell, wandering the country, meaning no harm."

Seeing himself as a counterinsurgent savior, Pyle strives to conjure a "third force"—between the commies and a crummy state—bankrolled by American overseers. Pyle knew what was best for other nations because he read all the right tomes about the joys of exporting democracy. Nothing ought to stand in the way of so gleamingly modern a cause. Pyle indeed anticipates Francis Fukuyama as a harbinger of the "end of history" thesis. This addled idealistic shock trooper dispenses plastic explosives to local contacts with the aplomb of a pharmacist filling diet pill prescriptions. Mass murder ensues but, Pyle reckons, like our Vietnam "rehabilitators," that it's entirely excusable because it's all in a good cause.

Greene mocked highly pedigreed American intruders who were not nearly as shrewd as the savvy Europeans, after slinking away or being tossed out of former colonies, still fancied themselves. Rereading *The Quiet American*, it seems an awfully British book— laced with a labored melancholic colonialist conceit— and thus it is, so far as the archetypal character Pyle is depicted, utterly wrong. It's not that men and women like Pyle do not exist. The war was waged by many people resembling the pathologically sincere Pyle, but the conflict was neither instigated nor run by them. Old-fashioned, cold-blooded *realpolitik* is practiced in much the same callous way the whole world over.

Peruse the *Pentagon Papers* and one finds American policy elites were every bit as inhumanly calculating as the most epicene European diplomats in their imperial heyday. Vietnam was by no stretch of the imagination a blunder, except in retrospect. Vietnam was neither a bungled war nor was it run by fools— unless vastly superior firepower makes fools of all who wield it. While the CIA had repudiated the "domino theory," it remained a means by which politicians nudged the impressionable public into crusades in faraway malarial lands. The Tonkin Gulf resolution literally was in Lyndon Johnson's back pocket long before the incidents allegedly took place in August 1964.

Did Pyle, or the model for Pyle, actually exist? Biographers of Graham Greene cagily say that Pyle was an amalgam of Greene's acquaintances, including Air Force general and CIA operative Edward Lansdale who, according to Daniel Ellsberg, enjoyed "playing dumb" and putting on a good ole boy persona whenever cornered by inquisitive journalists. Biographer Norman Sherry aptly remarks that Pyle resembled no one so much as an eager British public schoolboy of a certain vintage, the sort who manfully administered the Raj. Behold, however, a sterling sample of the American genus *Homo counterinsurgicus* at work: In Laos on 22 September 1961 a lieutenant colonel from the Military Assistance Advisory Group circulated a cheery memo on "civil assistance" which Lansdale, then assistant to the secretary of Defense on Special operations, praised. Pyle himself easily could have penned tidbits advising:

> Who to become acquainted with: political boss of district, High district judge, Police chief, religious leader, schoolmaster, leading businessmen, —Gather data on everyone else. Provide medical, education, sanitation, agricultural (crop rotation) support, transport, playground, tools, show American movies ("Avoid films which degrade us or are extremely sophisticated or complex")

> Initially your weapon is talk. It must be interesting, arousing, intelligent. You are a master salesman for the United States. —Oh yes don't remind them of the French. "Learn the customs of your region."

The sky is the limit in what you can achieve. You cannot make a new Laos in one day but it only takes one day to start. Now is the time to start beating the enemy at his own game—the winning of men's minds, emotions, and loyalty to the concept of freedom, justice, individual human rights, equality of opportunity, and a higher living standard.

Stirring stuff. But it's not as if ambitious officers were not available to do the unquestioned bidding of expeditious hard-nosed superiors. Here is the secret psyche of a leadership class bent on empire, though usually not that of most citizens. As for incorrigible idealists like the sprightly lieutenant colonel cited above, Shakespeare in his play *Julius Caesar* (as Chalmers Johnson reminds us), has cynical Octavian say of noble Brutus, "According to his virtue let us use him..."

Soldiers in Vietnam were misled systematically. Many believed that they were beating back the ravening Chinese Communist menace. Soviet soldiers in Afghanistan initially thought they were fighting to end feudalism there and to fend off external capitalist meddlers—and even to this day call the mujahideen "mercenaries." For bewildered Americans GIs, the fighting in the countryside grew so fierce that good will dissolved into indiscriminate rage toward "gooks," and, for a good many, toward their own government too. The discrepancies between the apple-cheeked beliefs we are asked to swallow and the real conduct of counter-insurgency operations were vast. A harrowing decade elapsed before most Americans, aghast, understood the myriad lies underpinning the Vietnam War.

Greene's "quiet American" was not only a condescending stereotype but a misleading one because

Pyle was primly unconcerned about what was in it for himself. What Greene's portrait missed was the firm anchoring of this febrile fanaticism in raw self-interest. Where the protagonist does begin to ring true—if we add the missing ingredient—is when observing neo-conservatives who gained control of the awesome machinery of an unelected government. Their Armani-suited ardor stemmed, unlike Pyle's, from unswerving power-seeking, as the authors of the Project for a New American Century clearly exhibit in that maniacal document. Unlike Pyle, it is not "nation-building" they seek but empire-building, everlasting warfare, and a quest for power without responsibility or accountability.

These implacable ideologues—Paul Wolfowitz, Douglas Feith, Richard Perle, John Bolton and others—knew what they stood to gain from a sweeping new Pax Americana. As jobs go, the role of imperial tribune beats that of scholar in the dusty book stacks any day. Even more gratifying, in the cultivated hysteria of 9/11, they eluded any serious questioning. Six key neoconservative figures have links to Israel's saber-toothed Likud Party, raising the legitimate question, which the media was too timid to ask, as to whose national interests they actually served.

They comprise the slick American equivalent of the grubby Taliban—true believers who never needed to defend crackpot ideas in an open forum, having been incubated in right-wing tycoons' foundations. I encountered some of them at a university where they formed a "happy few" filled with a heady glow of communing with ancient philosophers. One might have thought they trooped in and out of séances, not seminars. Formerly dismissed as a gang of "Conan the librarians," these bookish hoodlums suddenly were in charge, thanks to the Florida debacle of 2000 and the 9/11 attacks afterward. What distinguished them from Muslim fanatics were natty attire, ample resources, and language. They are identical spirits in their intense intolerance of other creeds. Pyle is more akin to this international wrecking crew, but the earnest spook might have recoiled at their glaring lack of humanity, humility, conscience or shame. The trouble now is that it is far from clear that President Obama's foreign policy staff—despite offering a more liberal frame for their actions—are one iota different.

\* \* \* \*

In Spring 1971, shortly after getting tear-gassed (as were I and thousands of others) at the Mayday anti-war demonstrations in Washington, DC, Daniel Ellsberg took his children on an automobile tour of revolutionary war battlefields. Ellsberg recalled,

> a bronze sign near the bridge at Concord that marks the graves of the British soldiers. I took a picture of the inscription on the plaque:
>
> *"They came three thousand miles to keep the past upon its throne."*

Nicaragua still was an invasion possibility in 1987—Irangate, fortunately, arose—when Ellsberg related that moment to a *Rolling Stone* interviewer. "Two hundred years later," Ellsberg concluded, "it's up to Americans to bring this country home again. If we succeed, there won't be a plaque in Nicaragua [or Iraq or Afghanistan] like the one in Concord, no plaque for

American soldiers who came three thousand miles and died." The sooner the US gets out of the business of counterinsurgency, the better. ◼

# Works Discussed:

*Full citations are available for download as a PDF via the Press' website, www.prickly-paradigm.com*

Ahmad, Eqbal. Theories of Counterinsurgency. *Bulletin of Concerned Asian Scholars* (1971)

Allen, George W. *None So Blind: a Personal Account of Intelligence Failure in Vietnam.* (Chicago: Ivan R Dee, 2001)

Appy, Christian G. (ed.) *Vietnam: The Definitive Oral History from all Sides.* (Suffolk: Ebury Press, 2006)

Baritz, Loren. *Backfire.* (New York: Morrow, 1985)

Bayly, Christopher and Tim Harper. *Forgotten Wars: The End of Britain's Asian Empire.* (London: Penguin, 2007)

Blaufarb, Douglas. *The Counterinsurgency Era: U.S. Doctrine and Performance, 1950 to the Present.* (New York: Free Press, 1977)

Bibring, Edward. The Concept of the Repetition Compulsion. *Psychoanalytic Quarterly* 12 (1943)

Blood, Jake. *Tet: Intelligence and the Public Perception of War.* (New York: Routledge, 2005)

Boyle, Richard. *Flower of the Dragon: The Breakdown of the US Army in Vietnam.* (New York: Ramparts Press 1972)

Brush, Peter. *Civic Action: The Marine Corps Experience in Vietnam, Part II.* (Library Science, University of Kentucky), p. 2. Fn 8. Brush cites the USMC, Small Wars Manual (Washington, D.C.: HQMC, 1940, 2nd ed). http://www3.iath.virginia.edu/sixties/HTML_docs /Texts/Scholarly/Brush_CAP_02.html

Buzzanco, Robert. *Masters of War.* (New York: Cambridge University Press, 1996)

----- and Lee Fought. David Shoup: Four Star Troublemaker. In David L. Andersen (ed.) *The Human Tradition in the Vietnam Era* (Lanham, MD: Rowman & Littlefield, 2000)

Cable, Larry. *Conflict of Myths: The Development of American Counterinsurgency Doctrine in the Vietnam War.* (New York: New York University Press, 1986)

Cobban, Helen. The role of mass incarceration in Counterinsurgency: A reflection on Caroline Elkins' Imperial reckoning in light of events. *Radical History* 96 (Fall 2006)

Colby, William E. with James McCarger. *Lost Victory: A Firsthand Account of America's Sixteen-Year Involvement in Vietnam.* (Chicago: Contemporary Books, 1989)

Chandler, Robert W. *War of Ideas: The US Propaganda Campaign in Vietnam.* (Boulder: Westview Press, 1981)

Darby, John. *Scorpions in a Bottle*. (London: Minority Rights Organization, 1997)

DePuy, General William. What we might have Done and Why we didn't do it. *ARMY* (February 1986)

Erhardt, William D. *In the Shadow of Vietnam*. (New York: McFarland & Co, 1991)

Elliot, David. *The Vietnamese War: Revolution and Social Change in the Mekong Delta, 1930-1978*. (New York: M. E. Sharpe 2003)

Ellsberg, Daniel. *Secrets: A Memoir of Vietnam and the Pentagon Papers*. (New York: Viking, 2002)

Falk, Richard A., Gabriel Kolko, and Robert Jay Lifton (eds. *Crimes of War*. (New York: Vintage Books, 1971)

Franklin, Bruce. *Vietnam and Other American Fantasies*. (Amherst: University of Massachusetts, 2000)

Freud, Sigmund. Why War? In *Standard Edition of the Complete Psychological Works of Sigmund Freud, Volume 22*. (London: Hogarth Press, 1966)

Geraghty, Tony. *The Irish War: The Hidden Conflict Between the IRA and British Intelligence*. (Baltimore: Johns Hopkins University Press, 2000)

Grant, Zalin. *Facing the Phoenix: The CIA and the Political Defeat of the United States in Vietnam*. (New York: Norton, 1991)

Gravel, Mike (ed.) *Pentagon Papers*. (Boston: Beacon Press, 1971)

Greene, Graham. *The Quiet American*. (London: Penguin, 1955)

Hunt, David and Jayne Werner. *The American War in Vietnam*. (Ithaca: Cornell University Press, 1993)

Hunt, David. Review of David Elliot, *The Vietnamese War*. *Critical Asian Studies* 35, 4 (2003)

Hunt, Richard A. *Pacification: America's Struggle for Vietnam's Hearts and Minds*. (Boulder: Westview Press, 1995)

Kennedy-Pipe, Caroline and Colin McInnes. The British Army in Northern Ireland: From Policy to Counter-terrorism. *Journal of Strategic Studies* 20, 2 (1997)

Kolko, Gabriel. *Vietnam: Anatomy of War*. (London: Allen & Unwin, 1986)

Knoebl, Kuno. *Victor Charlie: The Face of War in Vietnam*. (New York: Frederick Pager, 1967)

Laqueur, Walter. *Guerrilla: A Historical and Critical Study*. (Boston: Little, Brown, 1976)

Lifton, Robert J. *History and Human Survival*. (New York: Random House, 1970)

Long, Ngo Vinh. Land Reform? *Bulletin of Concerned Asian Scholars* (1971)

McGarry, Patrick and Brendan O'Leary. *Explaining Northern Ireland.* (Oxford: Basil Blackwell, 1995)

Moloney, Ed. *A Secret History of the IRA.* (London: Penguin, 2002)

Moyar, Mark. *Phoenix and the Birds of Prey: Counterinsurgency and Counterterrorism in Vietnam.* (Omaha: University of Nebraska, 2007, 2nd ed.)

----- *Triumph Forsaken: The Vietnam War 1954-65.* (New York: Cambridge University Press, 2006)

Nelson, Deborah. *The War Behind Me: Inside the Army's Secret Archive of Investigations.* (New York: Basic Books, 2008)

Orwell, George. Politics and the English Language. In *The Orwell Reader.* (New York: Harcourt Brace, 1961)

Petraeus, Lt General David H. Learning Counterinsurgency: Observations from Soldiering in Iraq. *Military Review* (January-February 2006)

Pilger, John. *Heroes.* (New York: Vintage, 2001)

Prochnau, William. *Once Upon a Distant War.* (New York: Vintage, 1995)

Race, Jeffrey. Vietnam Intervention: Systematic Distortion in Policy-making. *Armed Forces and Society* 2,3 (1976)

----- *War Comes to Long An.* (Berkeley: University of California Press, 1972)

Sahlins, Marshall. The Destruction of Conscience in Vietnam. In *Culture in Practice: Selected Essays.* (New York: Zone Books, 2000)

Sheehan, Neil. *A Bright Shining Lie.* (New York: Vintage, 1988)

Smith, Christian Stephen. *Resisting Reagan: The US Central American Peace Movement.* (Chicago: University of Chicago Press, 1996)

Sorley Lewis. *A Better War: The Unexamined Victories and Final Tragedy of America's Last Years in Vietnam.* (New York: Harcourt Brace & Company 1999)

Summers, Frank. The American Psychological Association, and the Involvement Of Psychologists at Guantanamo Bay. *Psychoanalysis, Culture and Society* 12 (April 2007)

Summers, Harry G. *On Strategy: A Critical Analysis of the Vietnam War.* (Novato, CA: Praesido Press, 1982)

Tang, Truong Nhu. *Viet Cong Memoir.* (New York: Harcourt, Brace, Jovanovich, 1985)

Tho, Brigadier General Tranh Dinh. Pacification. Prepared for Department of the Army (McLean, Virginia: General Research Corporation, 1977)

Trullinger, James. *Village at War.* (New York: Longman, 1980)

*U.S. Army/Marine Corps Counterinsurgency Manual.* (Chicago: University of Chicago Press, 2007)

Valentine, Douglas. *The Phoenix Program.* (New York: Morrow, 1990)

Viem, General Cao Van and Lt. General Dong Van Khuyen. *Reflections on the Vietnam War.* (Washington, DC: US Army Center of Military History, 1980)

Willbanks, James H. *The Tet Offensive: A Concise History.* (New York: Columbia University Press, 2007)

Windrow, Martin. *The Last Valley: Dien Bien Phu and the French Defeat in Vietnam.* (Cambridge, MA: Da Capo Press, 2004)

*The Winter Soldier Investigations: An inquiry into American War Crimes.* (Boston: Beacon Press, 1972)

Wood, Elisabeth. *Insurgent Collective Action and Civil war in El Salvador.* (Cambridge: Cambridge University Press, 2003)

Young, Marilyn. *The Vietnam Wars, 1945-1990.* (New York: Harper Perennial, 1991)

Also available from Prickly Paradigm Press:

*continued*